Narcissistic Parental Abuse Recovery

Empower Your Inner Child, Transform
Pain into Power, Reclaim Yourself,
and Rebuild Life After Trauma

By

Dr Arundhati Hoskeri

D1522463

Narcissistic Parental Abuse Recovery

Empower Your Inner Child, Transform Pain into Power, Reclaim Yourself, and Rebuild Life After Trauma

Publication: November 2024

All Rights Reserved

Copyright @ Dr Arundhati Hoskeri

Contact Email: authorarug@gmail.com

Please Visit Our Website

https://aruhoskeri.in

Table of Contents

Series: "The Dark Psychology Secrets."

"Narcissistic Parental Abuse Recovery" is the First Book in This Series.

"Dark Psychology Secrets" is a transformative book series that opens up **the hidden layers** of **emotional pain**, often buried under complex feelings and misunderstandings. Through each book, readers will find genuine guidance to identify emotional abuse, the scars it leaves, and the reasons that are often hard to recognize and take you toward healing. With real-life case studies, relatable scenarios, and practical insights, this series aims to illuminate and simplify what may feel confusing, isolating, or overwhelming.

This series isn't just about theories or academic insights; it's a proper support system. Every book offers actionable solutions to real situations people face in their relationships, friendships, and personal lives.

My intention is simple: to help people regain clarity, rebuild self-trust, and discover a path to emotional freedom. With books in this series, you'll find tools to face emotional struggles head-on and lead a true, resilient, and happy life.

Book Overview

- Are you struggling to understand the effects of growing up with a narcissistic parent/s?
- Do you find it hard to move past feelings of guilt, shame, or low self-worth?
- Are you ready to break free from patterns of unhealthy relationships and finally reclaim your life?

"Narcissistic Parental Abuse Recovery" is a compassionate guide for anyone dealing with the lingering impact of narcissistic abuse from a parent, especially a mother who is a primary caretaker.

This book is not about turning you against your parents or fostering resentment. Instead, it encourages self-reflection, understanding your behavior, and finding ways to heal to live a calm, happy life. Recovery is about setting boundaries, managing relationships healthily, and breaking harmful cycles.

Parents are our primary caregivers—they bring us into the world, look after us, and help us grow. Often, any hurt they cause may not be intentional; many may have suffered similar treatment themselves.

If you want to stop these cycles from continuing to the next generation and experience a happier life, it starts with deciding to take care of yourself.

It's natural to struggle with seeing our parents as narcissists, especially when they've cared for us, shown love, and provided for us. For children, this idea is almost impossible to understand. Even as adults, coming to terms with it is difficult, as it means accepting a painful reality. Yet healing requires us to face this truth.

We can't change what happened, but we can take steps to heal our emotional wounds and move forward. It isn't about assigning blame; it's about letting go of the hurt and finding peace for ourselves. Through healing, we can break these cycles and create healthier relationships in our own lives.

While physical wounds might leave visible scars, emotional wounds cut far deeper. Without attention, these inner wounds don't heal. Coping through distractions, like shopping, spending time with friends, or binging on shows or games, may offer brief relief, but it doesn't address the patterns of behavior caused by painful experiences. This approach is like covering an infected wound with a bandage—offering only a temporary fix.

Every person deserves happiness and peace, and only when we nurture it within ourselves can we share it with others. The first step is to understand our own patterns and why we act the way we do. Occasional difficult behavior doesn't necessarily indicate narcissism. Narcissism exists on a spectrum. At its extreme, some people may develop narcissistic personality disorder (NPD), a harmful and complex condition often requiring therapy and, sometimes, medication. **This book does not focus on NPD**, which falls at the highest end of this spectrum. Instead, it's for those experiencing milder forms of narcissistic traits or patterns, roughly ranging from 1 to 6 or 7 on a scale of 1 to 10.

This book aims to provide insights into these behavior patterns, which may be similar across people but affect each individual uniquely. By reading, you'll better understand these traits, how they appear in various ways, and their impact on those affected. With real-life examples, case studies, and research in the field, you will get a clearer picture of narcissistic traits.

It starts by exploring what narcissistic parental abuse means, unpacking traits and patterns often seen in narcissistic mothers and fathers. You'll gain insight into the roles that typically emerge in such families—like the scapegoat or golden child—and understand how sons and daughters are affected in distinct ways. It helps you recognize how manipulation, criticism, and constant control erode a child's self-worth and create lifelong scars with the help of case studies and real-life examples. It inspects the lasting wounds that emerge in adulthood.

Topics include the challenges of forming healthy relationships, the silent struggles with anxiety, depression, and low self-esteem, and the tendency to attract toxic partners. Through relatable examples and thoughtful analysis, the book makes these invisible wounds easier to understand and, ultimately, to heal.

The core of this book is about empowerment. You'll learn practical strategies for setting boundaries, acknowledging and validating your experiences, and healing the inner child within you. By reconnecting with your true self, finding your voice, and rebuilding your self-worth, you'll discover tools to live independently from the trauma of your past.

The book's final chapters guide fostering self-love, resilience, and emotional strength. With a focus on actionable advice and genuine encouragement,

Narcissistic Parental Abuse Recovery offers the support you need to build a life free from toxic cycles where you can thrive in relationships and find peace within. Start your journey to emotional freedom and lasting recovery today.

Preface

Today, narcissism is a widely discussed topic, thanks to the psychologists and therapists who are working hard to create awareness among common people to help them heal. Narcissism is not a by-product of modern times. It is as old as humanity.

We may deal with narcissists as our spouses/parents/ bosses/ children/friends, and we may not even realize it. We may feel these are just difficult people, but when we understand narcissism, we notice the classical set pattern of behavior.

Exploring this subject further may reveal that we have encountered such individuals. Still, we're unaware of the correct term for their behavior because no narcissist displays that tag on their forehead.

I have come across many narcissists ranging from mild to severe in my life, but fortunately, I managed to break free and heal myself with the support of my dear husband, who's a medical doctor.

And I have helped many to heal their emotional wounds. The urge to share my experience has been so strong that I have been thinking of writing on this subject for at least six years, but there was some hesitation.

--

The abundance of information on this subject on the internet and the extensive coverage in many books almost made me give up on the idea. Finally, I went ahead with my long pending project, and here I am, ready to publish this book.

Human behavior has always fascinated me. Ever since childhood, I have been a keen observer, curious to understand why people behave as they do. This natural curiosity only grew stronger when I entered the teaching profession. Suddenly, I found myself surrounded by thousands of students, their parents, and colleagues—each exhibiting unique behavior patterns.

It was like stepping into a vast laboratory where every interaction provided a new learning experience. I've learned over the years that no behavior occurs in isolation. A combination of inherited patterns, environmental influences, upbringing, and experiences shapes each person's actions and behavior.

For example, someone's confidence might result from supportive parents, while another's quietness might stem from a more restrictive household during childhood. But here's the intriguing part—behavior isn't static. It shifts, molds, and develops based on circumstances, emotions, and conscious efforts.

Unfortunately, individuals nurse emotional wounds and unpleasant thoughts and set behavior patterns of their childhood throughout their lives.

Understanding narcissistic behavior is essential for many reasons. On a personal level, it enhances self-awareness. When you know why you react to certain situations the way you do, it becomes easier to manage those reactions. Self-awareness can prevent impulsive actions, like snapping at a colleague or retreating into self-doubt, by offering insight into the triggers behind these reactions.

As the famous psychologist Carl Jung says, *"Until you make the unconscious conscious, it will direct your life, & you will call it fate."*

This fluidity of behavior opens up an exciting possibility: the ability to make intentional efforts toward consistency in one's actions and reactions. It's not about being rigid but about aligning your behavior with values that create harmony and balance.

When I pursued my Master's in Clinical Psychology, this understanding deepened. I realized that understanding behavior isn't just about observing others but also about looking inward and comprehending why we behave the way we do.

Something magical happened to me as I started helping others solve their problems. I began reflecting on my life journey, and I could identify harsh realities. Yes, I have interacted with so many narcissists at the workplace who tried to ruin my career in small or big ways, and I faced troubles in my personal life, too.

My father was a brilliant criminal lawyer and a genius. He was loving and gentle and spoke nicely when in a good mood. I owe a lot to him for expanding my intellectual horizons. But he had a terrible temper. I used to shiver when he would start screaming in a loud voice. He never used abusive language and never hit me, but he controlled me with his voice. I couldn't understand him and his mood swings, and I became an introvert as I grew older.

While growing up, I observed my mom being afraid of my dad's temper. Dad was an authority in our house, and Mom had no voice. Our life revolved around his moods, and I could never open my mouth when he was angry. This condition of giving in to authority percolated in my personality throughout, and when I started working, the bosses took advantage of my weakness.

I could not assert even when I was right, and they made a mountain out of a mole every time.

Two such authorities were grandiose, and I feared them and avoided confronting situations. It was my flight response to their aggression. Every time I was hurt or faced with their hostility, I used to get severe shoulder pain, my right trapezius muscle would get inflamed, and no painkillers or external applications would help. It was a psychosomatic condition, and that is when I explored natural health sciences such as Yoga, meditation, relaxation techniques, and home remedies to get relief.

Thankfully, my husband has the lion's share in making me who I am today. He's the mature, gentle, kind, and compassionate life partner to whom I'm ever grateful. It is a unique spiritual connection I have experienced with him. With his help, I came out of the trauma, healed myself, and started healing others.

Emotional wounds are excruciating and take longer to heal. I will accomplish my mission if I can heal at least a small percentage of people going through psychological pain.

I have always worked closely with the school's SEN department, which had a psychologist, counselor, and remediation teacher. As a teacher, I could get insights into the behavior problems of the students I taught that year.

When I became a principal, I could study all such cases in the entire school, from nursery to grade twelve. I always felt **we don't have problematic children, but all we have is problematic parents**, and this is so true!

I have seen many children having panic attacks during their assessments. In middle school, Rani was a bright kid, but during term-end exams and cycle tests, she'd invariably get cramps in her stomach and start throwing up. Bir, a high school kid, used to sleep and snore during the examinations.

Most children from broken homes were involved in bullying and physical fights. I never believed in punishing children and giving them a long lecture about behavior. My concern was to identify the root cause and help them rectify it.

Therefore, meeting the parents of children with mild to severe disruptive behavior was necessary.

I started meeting the parents and counseled them; I was shocked to find out a fact that many of the parents had mild to severe narcissistic tendencies or were victims of emotional abuse. It was an exciting revelation that such parents needed to heal themselves first to provide the emotional stability their children needed.

Parents or grandparents who were narcissistic or had some other mental conditions brought these adults up. Everyone's story was different, yet they had a common thread of narcissistic behavioral patterns. I stayed beyond school hours to help them.

As the news spread, more parents started seeing me for guidance. I did not have a clinic and wasn't a full-time counselor, so why and how did people trust me?

Maybe because, in India, seeing a psychologist or a counselor is still a bit of a taboo. People are not comfortable as they don't want to be labeled. They may have found it safer to consult me. When they came to me as my school parents, I advised them without charging them anything. It was my duty as a school head.

But when they wanted to come repeatedly and pay me for it, my conscience didn't permit me to use the school's premises for my activities, so I met them outside the school campus after working hours and then switched to online counseling sessions. They referred their relatives and friends to me; my clientele grew by word of mouth. Sometimes, I had to refuse because of the scarcity of time. However, some waited and came back to me.

When my near and dear ones learned about it, they passed remarks like, "Why do you have to get into it? Leave it to the experts in the field and enjoy your life." I replied to them with a smile and continued doing what I was doing because I was passionate about the field and enjoyed doing it.

Money has never been my only focus in whatever I do; I was passionate about counseling, and helping people overcome pain was so fulfilling. I could take a couple of weekday interactions and six sessions over the weekends. Spending time with my loving family was equally important. I have never administered any internal medications because I think I don't have expertise in that.

I'm an alternative medicine practitioner, trained in yoga and meditation, Neuro-Linguistic Programming (NLP), and a Past Life Regression Therapist (PLRT), and I believe in natural remedies. I have used these modalities as and when required.

The thought of writing this book has been haunting me for the last six years and ultimately finding its way to reach the readers.

Narcissistic behavior has set patterns, but how each faces such abuse is different, and also how therapists help each one break their cycle of pain and attain freedom is unique.

In this book, I have used research case studies, my own observations, and the cases I handled, but I have changed the names to maintain privacy.

I am sure that when you read about the instances or call them real-life stories, you may relate them to your own life and learn to break free and heal from them.

My goal is to create awareness about narcissism and help people come out of their past trauma and heal themselves completely. Knowing and understanding what you are going through is half the solution!

If you appreciate my sincere efforts, please comment on Amazon so that others in pain can get solace by reading this book.

I know I'm not the only one writing on Parental Narcissistic abuse, but my experiences of handling and healing the victims differ from other practitioners.

But please remember, merely reading this book will not help much. Learn from the stories, practice your learning, and be an action-taker. Please seek professional help if needed. You will realize, "**YOU ARE UNSTOPPABLE.**"

Introduction

"No man should bring children who are unwilling to persevere to the end in their nature and education."—Plato.

Human behavior is not static; it changes according to the situations, moods, and triggers. The rule of change -applies to our interactions. **If anything is permanent in life, it is the change**, I always say! We realize this if we study our own behavior and that of others. Several factors, such as a genetic inheritance of any mental disorder, family dynamics, neighborhood, peers, and society, shape our behavior and personality. Adults around us, such as parents, relatives, friends, teachers, and peers, influence us greatly.

And as I have observed, none of us are 100% perfect or normal. We may act peevish, withdrawn, selfish, submissive, or aggressive, and these traits may not be part of our personality. They may be situational. But when what we say and do starts affecting and hurting others, we must step back and check.

What is Narcissism?

Narcissism causes individuals to disregard the needs of those around them due to extreme self-involvement. While it's normal for everyone sometimes to show narcissistic behavior, true narcissists regularly disregard others and their feelings. In addition, they are oblivious to the consequences of their actions on other individuals.

It's worth mentioning that narcissism can be both a trait and a component of a more significant personality disorder. Narcissism is a spectrum, which means not all narcissists have NPD (Narcissistic Personality Disorder). Those classified as NPD are at the highest end of the spectrum, while others with narcissistic traits may fall on the lower end of the spectrum.

We don't know the exact cause of narcissism. Yet, it can be associated with:

Your surroundings: Your parents may have given you too much adoration or criticism that didn't match your actual experiences and achievements.

Genetics: There could be a connection between narcissism and your inherited characteristics, particularly personality traits.

Neurobiology: The link between your brain, behavior, and thinking is evident.

Signs of Narcissism are commonly associated with charm and charisma. It is common for negative behavior to not be immediately noticeable, particularly in relationships. Those with narcissistic tendencies prefer being around people who stroke their ego. To affirm their self-image, they establish relationships, even superficial ones.

Narcissism is a self-centered personality style with an excessive interest in one's physical appearance or image and too much preoccupation with one's own needs, often at the expense of others.

This obsession ranges from normal to abnormal expression of one's personality. When such persons become entirely self-absorbed, they may end up with a pathological illness like NPD -narcissistic personality disorder.

Are narcissists born or made?

Over the years, many have asked me, are narcissists born or made? You may be curious to know if narcissism stems from a genetic predisposition or if it is a characteristic that develops over time. As far as I have studied this trait and understood, it is a personality disorder that develops because of the environment and circumstances in which one grows and the styles of parenting they experience. The hallmark of narcissism is extreme selfishness. It's typical for all of us to show such behavior occasionally, but true narcissists do it regularly and have no empathy. We may not realize that narcissists are all around us until they regularly repeat their behavior patterns.

It is important to note that every narcissist may not end up with narcissistic personality disorder (NPD.)

The trait of narcissism is a broad spectrum. Individuals with NPD occupy the highest point on the spectrum, with others exhibiting similar traits placed at the lower end. However, it is not easy to deal with any degree of narcissism. Narcissists are the product of faulty or imbalanced parenting. Overindulgent or negligent parenting can completely distort children's personalities.

So, what do I mean by overindulgence? If children get too much attention, parents always praise and tell their kids that they are the best and unique, which can distort the kids' personalities. Such parents don't bother to correct their kids. They always cover up whenever their children mess up at home, school, or outside. They shower their children with empty praises, and the children constantly seek validation for whatever they do and quickly get upset when they don't get it. If one parent is a narcissist or both parents are narcissists, then their children may soon develop this trait - it is a fact that children learn by imitating the surrounding adults.

If the child does something wrong, and when the school brings such an incident to the parents' notice, parents may go to the school, shouting at the teacher or fighting with the school authorities instead of talking to the child and trying to correct their kids. Children immediately pick this up; the next time, they may not hesitate to mess up and learn to lie or manipulate. Suppose parents focus only on kids' achievements and provide them with everything even before the children ask and may fail to connect emotionally with their children. In that case, they can easily distort children's personalities.

For example, a working mother who has extended hours at work or a nonworking mother who is a social bee finds less or no time for her kids. They dump the kids with a caretaker or a house help or make them hop into various hobby classes and tuitions, which may negatively impact the children. Such kids no doubt may excel in studies or skills and are eager to please their parents with their medals or achievements that will make them feel good about themselves. But they may grow emotionally distant.

These children focus their self-esteem on seeking external validation. Such parents also push their children into events and competitions, click many pictures, video-graph the event, and proudly brag on social media and in their friend circle. Still, they may not be emotionally available to their children when needed. Such children develop narcissistic tendencies. They feel they are something special and others around them are not good enough. Children feel good when acknowledged, praised, and recognized; this constant craving for validation gradually sets in narcissistic tendencies.

Conversely, if children experience complete neglect, criticism, comparison, and ridicule from their parents and other adults, they may seek validation through constant achievements to prove them wrong. If children emotionally starve while growing up, they are prone to become insensitive to others' feelings, which may gradually lead to a lack of empathy. It is difficult for others to live or lead a life with narcissists, whether mild or moderate ones, and others need to develop a lot of coping mechanisms and learn to deal with narcissists.

Many narcissists either don't realize that they are narcissists or deny it to avoid a challenge to their identity. It becomes challenging to seek treatment for them because they feel completely normal while perceiving everyone else as wrong!

If narcissists develop NPD, it is impossible to live with them. NPD is a pathological that impairs a person's daily functioning. Their behavior causes friction in relationships because of a lack of empathy. While narcissism may not be hereditary, it can trigger and develop easily in individuals who have a family history of any genetic mental disorder like hysteria, BPD, schizophrenia, autism, attention deficit hyperactivity disorder (ADHD), and major depression.

NPD manifests as antagonism, grandiosity, constant attention-seeking, viewing everyone else as inferior, and people with NPD may be intolerant of disagreement or questioning. People with NPD have an inflated ego and unreasonably high sense of self-importance. They always crave attention, and they lack empathy. However, with this grandiose exterior, they often are insecure and have a poor sense of self-worth, so they get upset at the slightest criticism.

This book discusses how mild to moderate narcissism in parents emotionally abuses their children and how individuals can identify their hurts and wounds to heal themselves and lead a happier life.

This book does not discuss NPD and other mental illnesses because they are beyond its scope.

Chapter 1: Understanding Narcissistic Parental Abuse

"Control leaves no room for trust." —
Glennon Doyle.

Subunits:

- What is Narcissistic Parental Abuse?

- The Narcissistic Family Dynamics

- The Emotional Impact on Sons and Daughters

Roma walked into the living room where her 12-year-old son Raj and 8-year-old daughter Ria sat playing with their toys. **"Raj, stop being so lazy and help Ria clean up. I've told you a thousand times you're good for nothing!"** she snapped, barely glancing in Ria's direction.

Ria looked up, waiting for her mother's affection, but instead, Roma turned to her and said, **"You always need someone's help, don't you? When will you stop being so useless?"**

It was just another typical day in Raj and Ria's life. On the surface, it may seem like Roma was having a bad day or being harsh. But this behavior was far from occasional—it was a pattern. One where Roma consistently tore down her children, making them feel inadequate while demanding their loyalty and admiration.

In her world, only one person mattered—Roma herself. Roma is a narcissistic mother. Her husband, John, always supported her and often criticized his children to support his wife.

What is Narcissistic Paternal Abuse?

Narcissistic parental abuse occurs when a mother or father with narcissistic traits emotionally, mentally, and sometimes physically abuses their children to maintain control, assert their superiority, and fulfill their emotional needs at the expense of the children. This type of abuse leaves deep scars on children, affecting their self-esteem, relationships, and sense of identity well into adulthood. But before we dig deeper into what this abuse looks like, let's first understand: What is a narcissistic parent?

The Narcissistic Parent

A narcissistic mother isn't just a mom, and such a father is not just a dad who is occasionally harsh or who sets high expectations. They have a persistent pattern of behavior that centers around themselves. Everything they do is about protecting their self-image, getting admiration, and controlling their family. Their children aren't individuals in their eyes—they are extensions of themselves or obstacles that challenge their sense of perfection. Narcissistic parents lack empathy, and their world revolves around their needs, desires, and emotions. Their children exist to serve those needs. If a child tries to step outside this role, the narcissistic parent quickly puts them in their place—often through **manipulation, guilt-tripping, or outright criticism.**

Common Traits of Narcissistic Parents

Lack of Empathy

One of the most defining characteristics of narcissistic parents is their inability to empathize with their children truly. They may pretend to care when it benefits or makes them look good, but they don't connect deeply with their children's feelings.

For example, Raj felt hurt after a bad day at school and came home with a long face. His mother, Roma, may quickly dismiss his feelings and say, "Well, I went through much harder times when I was your age, so stop being so dramatic." Rather than validating his feelings, she diminished them.

Controlling Behavior

Everything must go according to her plans, or there will be consequences. A narcissistic mother controls her children's lives—what they wear, who they interact with, and even how they feel.

Raj might want to hang out with his friends, but Roma would guilt-trip him by saying, "I need you at home. You're so selfish for wanting to leave me alone." It's never about what Raj wants—it's always about her needs.

It reminds me of an incident from several years ago. During our school's dress rehearsal for the annual day concert, all the children were ready to go on stage when ten-year-old Sia realized she had forgotten her headgear at home.

Her class teacher called her mother from the school office. Since Sia's house was just a short walk away, her mother brought the headgear, but when she arrived, she angrily pulled Sia aside and started hitting her in front of everyone.

The poor girl silently cried, unable to defend herself against her much bigger mom. The teachers quickly stepped in and pulled Sia away.

The mother got annoyed because she was heading to a kitty party, and she was disturbed. She came herself to teach a lesson to Sia. The family was wealthy, and any of their servants could have quickly brought the headgear.

Later, we discovered Sia was the youngest of four daughters, and her mother had always wanted a son. Because of this, Sia faced both physical and emotional abuse from her mother.

Recently, I heard Sia got married, but her husband also physically abused her. After two years of marriage, she divorced him and is now single and working.

Envy and Competition

Even though it may sound odd, a narcissistic parent can harbor envy towards their children. If the children begin to shine, they might feel threatened. For instance, when Raj won a school sports award, John made an offhand comment like, "I was winning awards like that all the time at your age. It's nothing special." Instead of celebrating Raj's success, he belittled it, fearing that his son's achievements might overshadow his own.

Conditional Love

In a healthy relationship, parents' love is unconditional. But with narcissistic parents, love is often transactional. If you do what they want, you get their approval. If you don't, you face their wrath or cold indifference. Raj might bend backward, trying to please Roma or John, but they could withdraw their affection or lash out when he doesn't meet their expectations.

Playing the Victim

Narcissistic mothers are experts at playing the victim. If something goes wrong, it's never their fault. Narcissistic mothers manipulate the truth to make themselves appear like victims.

Let's say Ria calls out her mother's unfair treatment. **"I've dedicated my life to you, and this is how you show your gratitude,"** Roma might say in response. You're so ungrateful." This tactic deflects attention away from her bad behavior and puts the child in a position of guilt.

Gaslighting

Narcissistic parents are skilled manipulators and often use gaslighting to distort reality and confuse their children. They may deny things they said or did, making the child question their memory and perception.

For example, John may yell at Raj and call him "stupid." Later, when Raj confronts him, he may say, "I never called you stupid. You're imagining things. Why are you always so sensitive?"

Patterns of Narcissistic Abuse

These are the traits that translate into abusive patterns in narcissistic parenting.

Emotional Manipulation

Narcissistic parents are experts in using guilt, fear, and shame to control their children. They might cry about how "nobody loves them" or how "everyone takes them for granted" when their children don't cater to their needs. Over time, their children may put their parents' emotional needs above their own to avoid feeling guilty or blamed.

Triangulation

A common tactic used by narcissistic mothers is triangulation, where they pitch siblings against each other. Roma may praise Ria for being more "obedient" than Raj, or she may complain to Ria about how difficult Raj is, creating competition and conflict between them.

This distracts her children and ensures they don't unite against her. It also maintains her control position, where each child seeks her favor and approval.

Projection

Projection is when the narcissistic parent attributes their negative traits to their children. If John feels insecure, he might accuse Raj of being "selfish" or "arrogant." This way, he avoids facing his own flaws and makes Raj feel like he is the problem.

Emotional Neglect

Although narcissistic parents may shower their children with material things or perform acts that make them seem like "wonderful parents," they often neglect their children's emotional needs. Raj and Ria may never hear words of genuine love or support. They might pay little attention to their accomplishments or downplay them while emphasizing their failures. Over time, they may begin to believe they are not worthy of love unless they constantly meet their parent's impossible standards.

Smothering and Enmeshment

On the other end of the spectrum, some narcissistic parents may appear overly involved in their children's lives, blurring boundaries and making it difficult for the children to develop a sense of independence. Raj might feel suffocated by John's constant involvement, unable to make his own decisions because his father always tells him what to do.

John's need to control and possess his children makes it hard for Raj or Ria to form a sense of self outside their parents' influence.

The Lasting Impact

The effects of narcissistic parental abuse often carry into adulthood. Raj and Ria might struggle with low self-esteem, constant self-doubt, or a deep fear of failure. They may attract narcissistic partners, unknowingly repeating the same abusive patterns. Because no one taught them to value themselves, they might become people-pleasers, constantly seeking validation from others.

Healing from narcissistic parental abuse is a journey, and the first step is recognizing the patterns. As adults, children of narcissistic mothers and fathers can learn to set boundaries, seek therapy, and start reclaiming their sense of self.

Remember, your parent's narrative does not define you. You have the power to write your own story.

The Narcissistic Family Dynamics

Family is often associated with love, support, safety, and value. But in a narcissistic family, this picture couldn't be further from reality.

Control, manipulation, and favoritism drive the dynamics in a narcissistic family, with carefully assigned and enforced family roles serving the needs of the narcissistic parent. The children in these families often grow up feeling confused, hurt, and lost, each carrying the burden of a role they never asked for.

We will examine how narcissism influences family dynamics and the typical roles found in these environments.

Roles in a Narcissistic Family

In a narcissistic family, the parent assigns each child a role, whether they are aware of it. These roles help the narcissistic parent maintain control and ensure that their needs come first.

The two most common roles are the 'Golden Child' and the 'Scapegoat,' though other supporting roles, like the Invisible Child or Enabler, exist.

The Golden Child

The Golden Child is the star of the family, at least in the eyes of the narcissistic parent. The narcissists perceive this child as a reflection of their own perfection. The golden child is the chosen one who can do no wrong. But being the Golden Child comes with a heavy price.

Take Samir, for example. In his family, his mother, a textbook narcissist, placed him on a pedestal from an early age. Whenever he accomplished something noteworthy, whether a high grade or a sports victory, she proudly paraded him in front of relatives, exclaiming, "Witness my son, the upcoming sensation. There were constant reminders to him about his extraordinary nature and the unmatched qualities he possessed within the family.

There was no room for Samir to make mistakes. His mother would flip the script if he slipped, even just a little. "How could you let me down like this? You're not trying hard enough!" she'd say—the praise he was used to quickly turned into harsh criticism. The pressure to live up to his mother's impossible expectations was crushing.

As time passed, Samir began to think that his value was based only on his accomplishments. He never felt free to express his emotions or ask for help because his role was to be perfect. And deep down, he struggled with constant anxiety, always afraid of falling from grace.

The Scapegoat

The family views the Scapegoat as the villain in their dynamic, contrasting the Golden Child, who is seen as the hero. The family attributes anything and everything that goes wrong to the Scapegoat. This child serves as a target for the narcissistic parent's anger and frustration.

Let's look at Kavya's story. Her older sister, Neha, was the Golden Child, while Kavya was the Scapegoat. Whenever something went wrong—whether it was a minor family issue or a big one—Kavya was the one who got blamed. "If only you were more like Neha," her mother would say, "then this family wouldn't have so many problems."

Even if Kavya did something right, it was never enough. When she earned an award at school, her mother responded, "Well, Neha's won bigger prizes, but I guess this is okay.

Kavya believed she could never meet expectations, regardless of her efforts. She became the family's emotional punching bag, absorbing the frustration that her mother didn't want to take out on the Golden Child.

Kavya's role as the Scapegoat left her feeling isolated and resentful. She grew up believing she was the problem, even when it was clear her mother was the one causing the family chaos. Kavya learned to expect rejection and mistreatment in relationships, which impacted her adult life, leading her to accept toxic friendships and romantic partners.

The Invisible Child

In some families, there's also an Invisible Child. This child flies under the radar, receiving little positive or negative attention. While this might seem like a better deal than being the Scapegoat, it's just as damaging in its own way.

Take Rohan, for instance. His parents were so focused on his older brother, the Golden Child, and his younger sister, the Scapegoat, that Rohan often felt he didn't exist. When he came home from school, no one asked about his day. When Rohan needed help with homework, his parents were too busy managing the drama between his siblings to notice. Rohan felt ignored, as though he wasn't important enough to warrant attention.

As a result, Rohan grew up feeling invisible. He struggled with self-esteem because he never got validation from his parents. In relationships, he tended to shrink into the background, afraid to assert his needs because he believed they didn't matter.

The Enabler

The Enabler plays a crucial role in maintaining the narcissistic family dynamic. This person, often the other parent or sometimes even one of the children, reinforces the narcissistic parent's behavior. They excuse the narcissist's actions, downplay the abuse, and ensure that everyone follows the narcissist's rules.

In Kavya's family, her father was the Enabler. He would see how her mother treated Kavya unfairly but rarely stepped in to defend her. When Kavya came to him upset, he'd say things like, "Your mother's had a tough day; don't take it personally," or "You know how she gets. Just try to stay out of her way."

This kind of enabling allows the narcissist to continue their abuse unchecked. It also teaches the children that the narcissist's feelings matter more than their own. The Enabler may give the impression of maintaining peace, but they are actually contributing to the dysfunction.

The Impact of Narcissistic Family Roles

The roles in a narcissistic family don't just disappear when the children grow up. The emotional scars and unhealthy patterns often follow them into adulthood, affecting their relationships, self-worth, and mental health.

Impact on the Golden Child

Their belief system makes them feel immense pressure to succeed, as their self-worth is tied to their achievements. They might have difficulty accepting failure or criticism and could become narcissistic themselves, having learned that they are "special" and deserving of admiration. The Golden Child, like Samir, may struggle with perfectionism as an adult.

On the other hand, some Golden Children eventually recognize the dysfunction they were part of and feel immense guilt for having been favored. They may struggle to form healthy relationships, unsure how to connect without seeking constant approval.

Impact on the Scapegoat

The Scapegoat, like Kavya, often grows up feeling inadequate and unworthy. They may internalize the blame and criticism they receive and struggle with low self-esteem, anxiety, and depression.

They may become manipulators and secretly hate their golden child siblings. As adults, they may find themselves drawn to toxic relationships where they are mistreated because that's what feels familiar.

However, Scapegoats are also more likely to become the "truth-tellers" in the family. They're the ones who see the narcissist's behavior for what it is and may eventually break free from the cycle of abuse. Though it's a tough road, many Scapegoats learn to heal and rebuild their self-worth through therapy and self-reflection.

Impact on the Invisible Child

The Invisible Child, like Rohan, might continue feeling overlooked in adulthood. They may struggle to assert themselves in relationships and express their needs.

Due to constant neglect, they frequently experience a disconnection from their own emotions. As adults, they might avoid conflict or try to stay out of the spotlight, which can hinder their personal and professional growth.

Freeing From Narcissistic Family Dynamics

Healing from the narcissistic family dynamics isn't easy, but it is possible. The first step is recognizing the roles you were placed in and understanding how they have affected you. Therapy can be incredibly helpful in unpacking these dynamics and learning healthier ways to relate to others.

Whether you were the Golden Child, the Scapegoat, the Invisible Child, or an Enabler, understand that your worth goes beyond your assigned role. Free yourself from the narcissistic family dynamics and construct a life rooted in your genuine value rather than the distorted self-image imposed by the narcissist.

It's important to understand these roles were crafted to serve the narcissist, not you. You have the power to step out of these roles and build a life that reflects who you truly are.

The Emotional Impact on Sons and Daughters of Narcissistic Mothers

When it comes to maternal abuse from a narcissistic mother, both sons and daughters suffer deeply, but they often experience and internalize that abuse differently.

Narcissistic mothers, being highly manipulative and emotionally unavailable, create an environment where children feel trapped in roles and expectations that can leave lifelong emotional scars. The way sons and daughters react to and cope with maternal abuse tends to vary, shaped by cultural norms, gender expectations, and the unique dynamics within the family. Let's explore how maternal abuse affects sons and daughters, using examples to understand their experiences better.

Sons of Narcissistic Mothers

A narcissistic mother often has a precise vision of what her son should be like. Sons are often viewed as an extension of the mother, expected to embody her ideals of strength, success, and perfection. Meanwhile, these boys are subjected to emotional manipulation, kept at a distance, and seldom able to show vulnerability. For many sons, the relationship with a narcissistic mother is a tug-of-war between her praise and harsh criticism.

The Pressure to Be "Perfect"

Arjun's mother always focused on his achievements, including getting top grades, excelling in sports, and behaving impeccably in front of others. On the surface, it might have looked like she was proud of him. **But this pride was conditional.**

If Arjun scored 98 on a test, his mother wouldn't congratulate him. Instead, she'd say, "Why wasn't it 100? It would help if you worked harder. How do you think this makes me look?" For Arjun, nothing was ever enough. As a result, Arjun grew up feeling like his worth depended solely on his achievements. He internalized his mother's criticism and believed he wasn't good enough. Over time, this led to anxiety and perfectionism in his adult life. Arjun always chased approval but never felt truly worthy of love, whether at work, in friendships, or in romantic relationships.

Emotional Suppression

Sons of narcissistic mothers also often face intense emotional suppression. Mike had a mother who would dismiss his emotions whenever he was upset. Mike's mother would dismiss his feelings by saying, "Stop crying, boys don't cry," whenever he was hurt or sad. You need to toughen up." This constant invalidation of his emotions made Mike believe that showing vulnerability was a weakness. As Mike grew older, he found it difficult to express his feelings. Mike became emotionally distant, often retreating into himself when he was struggling. In relationships, Mike's partners would tell him that he seemed emotionally unavailable or cold, but he didn't know how to open up. He learned from his mother to keep emotions hidden rather than sharing them.

Daughters of Narcissistic Mothers

Daughters often bear the brunt of a narcissistic mother's manipulation very differently. While sons might face pressure to achieve and be perfect, narcissistic mothers frequently subject daughters to a toxic web of comparison, control, and competition. Narcissistic mothers can be incredibly critical of their daughters, undermining their self-worth at every turn while also being envious of them.

The Battle for Control and Identity

Let's look at the story of Meera, whose mother constantly competed with her, especially as she grew older. Meera's mother often made subtle comments like, "You should wear something more flattering; that doesn't suit your body type," or "When I was your age, I had boys lined up to date me, but you're so picky." These comments chipped away at Meera's confidence, making her doubt her appearance, choices, and worth.

Meera's mother also controlled many aspects of her life, from what she wore to who she was allowed to spend time with. Meera's mother questioned or overridden every decision she made, leaving her powerless. Even as an adult, Meera found it hard to make independent choices, constantly second-guessing herself because she had been conditioned to believe that she couldn't trust her judgment.

The Envy and Sabotage

In some cases, narcissistic mothers are outright envious of their daughters. This was the case for Priya. As Priya grew into a confident young woman, her mother's jealousy became more pronounced. If Priya received a compliment, her mother would immediately find a way to tear her down. If Priya wore a new dress, her mother would say, "That color washes you out," if Priya shared good news about a promotion, her mother would say, "Well, let's see if you can keep up with the pressure."

Priya's mother didn't want her to succeed or feel good about herself because, in the narcissist's mind, only she could shine. The constant belittling and passive-aggressive comments made Priya feel small, unsure of her worth, and always seeking external validation.

As an adult, Priya often found herself in relationships where her partners were controlling or dismissive, echoing the toxic dynamic she had with her mother.

The truth is narcissists do not realize they are damaging their children. Their feelings are subtle, and they may not ponder over their behavior. Such parents believe they are doing everything for the good of their children; they think it is normal, and their parents behaved the same with them when they were growing up.

Once, Jane, the mother of a seventh grader, came to see me on her own. I had not called her; her daughter, Lara, was a well-behaved girl who was above average in academics and participated in co-curricular activities.

Jane loved her only daughter and provided everything for her. She took her studies and worked hard at home and in the office to live a decent life. Then what was her problem? Suddenly, when Lara began puberty and started looking beautiful, Jane silently hated her daughter. She would use cuss words, curse her, get irritated, and overreact to whatever Lara did. The daughter was a bit disturbed, but it was eating up Jane, and she was so confused about the sudden change in her behavior.

There was an interesting revelation as I guided her through self-exploration through worksheets, journaling, and deep relaxation. Jane confessed that this is exactly how her mother behaved with her when she was thirteen! Her father was uncaring and never bothered to provide even basic amenities for the family. He had multiple extramarital affairs. Jane's mother had to look after her five children, and she had no choice but to get into a relationship with a man who helped her financially to some extent.

She was going through a lot of shame and guilt and expressed her frustration on Jane, the eldest daughter. She reacted, cursed Jane using abusive language, and constantly nitpicked her. Even as a child, Jane used to tell herself that she would have only one kid, treat her child kindly, and shower her with love and affection.

She was doing it, but when her daughter was fifteen, Jane's wounds and hurts experienced in her childhood unconsciously surfaced. But thankfully, she could detect it and seek help. No mother intentionally harms her children, and it is often the trauma they went through during childhood and their unhealed wounds that influence their behavior. Recognizing our own behavior is very important to overcome the wrong patterns.

Sons and Daughters Cope Differently

Though both sons and daughters experience emotional damage from their narcissistic mothers, the coping mechanisms they develop tend to differ, shaped by societal norms around gender.

Sons Strive for Perfection, Hiding Vulnerability

Sons like Arjun and Mike often cope by striving for perfection and burying their emotional needs. Society tells boys to be strong, unemotional, and successful, and narcissistic mothers reinforce this message. As a result, many sons of narcissistic parents become high achievers, always trying to prove their worth through accomplishments. They may also become emotionally distant, finding it hard to express vulnerability because they've learned that emotions are something to be ashamed of.

In some cases, sons may take on narcissistic traits themselves. Being raised to believe that they are unique, superior, and destined for greatness can lead sons to develop narcissistic traits themselves. It can result in unhealthy relationships where they demand admiration and struggle with empathy, echoing the behavior of their narcissistic mothers.

Daughters: People-Pleasing and Struggling with Self-Worth

Daughters, on the other hand, often become chronic people-pleasers. Having spent years trying to gain their mother's approval, they carry this need into other areas of their lives. Such an attitude often has difficulty setting boundaries and saying no because they fear rejection or disapproval.

Meera was referred to me when she was in grade five. Despite being capable, she hesitated to participate in the class or events. She had internalized the message that she wasn't good enough after being told so, directly or indirectly, leading to a struggle with self-worth. We constantly counseled this kid three times a week, and she took almost five years to overcome this feeling of inadequacy. Many daughters of narcissistic mothers spend years in therapy, working through the deep-seated belief that they are unworthy of love and respect.

Some daughters may also develop codependent tendencies, entering relationships where they care for others at the expense of their own needs. They might choose partners who are emotionally unavailable or narcissistic, perpetuating the toxic cycle they experienced with their mother.

Breaking Free from Parental Abuse

Whether you're a son or a daughter, the emotional impact of having a narcissistic parent is profound and long-lasting. But healing is possible. Recognizing the abuse for what it is—the narcissist's need for control and validation, not a reflection of your worth—is the first step. Therapy can be beneficial, offering a safe space to explore feelings, set boundaries, and rebuild one's sense of self.

Sons must understand that expressing vulnerability is acceptable and their accomplishments do not determine their value. Daughters might need to work on self-compassion and recognizing their inherent value independent of their mother's approval. Both sons and daughters must reclaim their identities, separate from the roles their mothers imposed on them.

The journey is not easy, but it's worth it. Sons and daughters of narcissistic mothers deserve to live lives free from the emotional chains of their childhoods. By acknowledging the abuse and committing to healing, they can break the cycle and build healthier, more fulfilling relationships with themselves and others.

Case Study: The Impact of Parental Narcissism on Children's Psychological Development. (2015)

Brummelman et al. (2015) conducted a well-known longitudinal study on the impact of narcissistic parenting on children, tracking their self-esteem and mental health development over several years. The research discovered that children with narcissistic parents, especially mothers, had a much higher chance of developing low self-esteem, anxiety, depression, and difficulties with emotional control.

Research pointed out that narcissistic mothers see their children as part of themselves, which can result in love being tied to the child's accomplishments. These youngsters are often under pressure to meet unrealistic standards and tend to feel inadequate when they don't meet them. The emotional baggage causes sustained harm to their psychological health, leading to challenges with self-esteem that persist into adulthood.

Healing Focus: The study suggests that children of narcissistic parents benefit greatly from therapeutic approaches focused on rebuilding self-esteem, separating their identity from their parent's expectations, and learning self-compassion. Therapy that encourages unconditional self-acceptance is critical for healing.

Chapter 2: The Deep Wounds of Childhood

"It is easier to build strong children than to repair broken men." — *Frederick Douglass.*

Subunits

- The process of self-worth and identity formation
- Absorbing guilt, shame, and fear internally
- Growing Up in Survival Mode

The Process of Self-Worth and Identity Formation

The continuous manipulation and criticism can harm a child's self-worth. The constant manipulation and criticism in narcissistic families can crush a child's identity. The child develops uncertainty about their identity, and their self-esteem becomes linked to pleasing others, particularly their narcissistic parent.

Narcissistic parenting marked the upbringing of Bina and Ami, resulting in remarkably similar experiences and distorted self-perception.

Bina, the unassuming pleaser

Bina was always obedient and followed the rules. She spoke softly, followed orders, and put in an effort to make her mother happy. Her mother, a typical narcissist, ensured Bina never felt adequate. Bina's mom publicly praised her daughter's academic achievements, making it difficult for others to see the truth. However, the situation was different behind closed doors.

Excited about her top marks on the math test, Bina rushed home one evening to show her mother. With a glowing expression, she gave me the paper. Her mom barely looked at it.

"You got a 95? What went wrong with the other 5%?" her mother inquired, raising an eyebrow. Bina's spirits plummeted. She had worked so hard, hoping for recognition or even a hug. Yet, she couldn't shake the feeling that she had let herself down. Her mother's words repeatedly played in her head: What happened to the other 5%?

It wasn't an isolated event. Regardless of Bina's achievements, others always considered them insufficient. No matter how much she pitched in, her mother always found something to criticize: "The dishes are still wet."Are you incapable of doing anything correctly?" Bina learned that her worth was always up for debate—hanging by a thread, and she felt she had to earn it repeatedly.

The constant criticism influenced Bina's self-perception. Her confidence in her own judgment faded away. She filtered every decision she made with the question, Will mom approve? It continued well into her adult years.

Bina's tendency to doubt herself at work constantly led her to seek approval from her bosses and colleagues.

She would do anything to avoid relationship conflict and go to great lengths to please her partner, fearing he would leave if she weren't flawless. Bina became a people-pleaser who tried to avoid criticism and rejection. Her fragile self-worth relied on others' approval, particularly her mother's.

In public, Bina's mom made sure she had created an excellent image for herself, that of a hardworking, loving, and caring parent. She was helpful to her friends and neighbors, spoke highly of her family, and praised her daughter. Her mother's duel behavior confused Bina, who ended up believing her mother was always good, and the problem was her own inadequacy.

Bina's mom depicts the traits of a communal narcissist who is wise and manipulative.

Amit Was The rebel who couldn't flee.

Amit's experience was unique. Bina adapted by being submissive and obedient, while Amit resisted his self-centered father. Amit's father was strict and excessively judgmental, anticipating him to pursue a legal career like him. Amit had no interest in studying law. He had a strong affinity for art and dreamt of being an artist. Amit's conflicting vision with his father's led to him being deemed a "disappointment" from a young age.

"Making a living by drawing cartoons and landscapes is impossible," his father would sneer. You have so much potential that you're not harnessing.

Despite Amit's best attempts to convey his passion, it was futile. His dad brushed off his dreams, considering them childish fantasies. Amit stopped attempting to please him and adopted the "problem child" role instead. Without approval, he sought attention, even if it was negative.

In his innermost self, Amit believed he was a failure. His father's words reverberated in his mind: You're not living up to your full potential. No matter how talented Amit was in art, the praise from his teachers and admiration from his friends didn't make a difference.

The only opinion that seemed to matter was his father's; according to him, Amit would never amount to anything.

Such negatively affected his sense of self. Throughout his upbringing, he felt inadequate, convinced that his actions would never meet the standards of excellence. No matter where Amit went to pursue his career, his father's voice always stayed with him.

While working as a graphic designer, he couldn't help but wonder if his father had been right all along. Am I genuinely squandering my capabilities? This nagging doubt tainted his work, relationships, and daily life.

While he showed defiance on the surface, Amit harbored the same emotional scars as Bina. Continuous criticism Amit received formed his identity—such a belief of being inadequate limited his success, even in areas where he should have prospered.

The Influence of Manipulation and Criticism

Although Bina and Amit handled their narcissistic parents differently, they both ended up with a distorted sense of self. Bina's people-pleasing and Amit's rebellion were responses to constant criticism and manipulation. Because of their parents' frequent changes in expectations, they could not establish a stable identity.

Narcissistic parents have a way of controlling how their children see themselves. Bina always felt her worth depended on her performance because her mother's approval was elusive. Amit thought he could never measure up because his father's disapproval overshadowed his passions.

The manipulation persists even after the children move out. It haunts their thoughts, impacts their relationships, and guides their actions. Bina's lack of confidence in her decision-making persisted into adulthood, causing her to constantly seek approval from others. Despite his talent, Amit couldn't escape the belief that his passions were worthless, hindering his progress.

Emotional Abuse Recovery is Possible

Recovering from emotional manipulation is possible, although it is a time-consuming process. Bina, for instance, ended up seeking therapy, discovered how to establish boundaries, and is no longer seeking her mother's approval.

She developed her self-worth by focusing on her values and disregarding others' opinions. Over several years, she had to undo the belief that she had to be flawless to be loved.

The way Amit healed was distinctively different. He experienced a phase of intense anger as he came to understand the profound impact of his father's words on him. However, Amit discovered a means to regain his identity through art. He began making artwork that conveyed his pain and frustration, gradually rebuilding confidence in his abilities. His sense of success was no longer dependent on his father's approval.

Bina and Amit's stories show that escaping the control of narcissistic parents is possible despite the significant harm they can cause. They rebuilt their identities by recognizing manipulation and learning self-trust, no longer defined by past criticism.

Children like Bina and Amit, raised by narcissistic parents, often face challenges with their self-worth. Regardless of whether they become people-pleasers or rebels, the harm is identical.

They feel like they are never enough because of years of criticism and manipulation affecting their self-perception. Yet, with awareness and assistance, they can heal, reclaim their authentic self, and realize that someone else's validation does not determine their worth.

Absorbing Guilt, Shame, and Fear Internally

These Toxic Emotions Manifest and Linger Into Adulthood.

When children grow up in toxic environments, particularly with narcissistic parents, they often internalize emotions like guilt, shame, and fear. These emotions are harmful because they don't just fade away as the children grow older. Instead, they linger, shaping how these people see themselves and interact with the world.

Cases of Alia and Ajay, who carried the weight of guilt, shame, and fear from childhood into their adult lives.

The guilt burden of being the "good" daughter

Alia's family assigned her the responsibility of caring for them. Her mother frequently reassured her, saying, "You're the dependable daughter I can count on." Alia's mother would make her feel responsible for everything that went wrong. If her younger brother got in trouble at school, her mother would say, "Why didn't you teach him better?" If her father came home angry, her mother would ask Alia, "Can't you help keep the peace around here?"

Gradually, Alia believed she was responsible for everything. She wasn't only the dutiful daughter but the glue that united the family. If any mishaps occurred, it was because of her lack of effort. Her internal guilt directly resulted from the constant messaging. Even as a kid, she had the persistent feeling of being at fault for every family conflict or issue. When Alia was 14, her father lost his job. Everyone was going through a challenging period, and the tension at home was unbearable. Her mother angrily blamed her, saying, "Maybe if you were more helpful, your father wouldn't be so stressed. "Maybe I honestly should have put in more effort," Alia pondered, even though she was confused about how she was responsible for her father's job loss.

This guilt stayed with Alia well into adulthood. As an adult, she was the person everyone relied on—at work, in her friendships and romantic relationships. She was always the **"problem fixer"** who ensured everything was okay. But deep down, she never felt she was doing enough. No matter how hard she tried, there was always this nagging feeling that if something went wrong, it was somehow her fault. In relationships, this guilt made her afraid to say no. If her husband was upset, she felt it was her job to fix it, even if she had done nothing wrong. She often apologized for things that weren't her fault to keep the peace. Alia had become so used to feeling responsible for others' emotions that she lost track of her needs.

Case Study: The Father Who Never Listened (2011)

Narcissistic Fathers and Their Impact on Emotional Regulation in Children

Miller et al. carried a significant study on the emotional development of children with narcissistic fathers out (2011). According to the research, narcissistic fathers tend to ignore their children's emotions, dismiss their feelings, and prioritize their own needs in interactions. This results in long-lasting problems with managing emotions.

In this case study, we encounter "Paul," a man in his 40s who has grappled with anger management issues for many years. Paul's father was very critical, never letting him show his emotions without facing ridicule or punishment. Consequently, Paul learned to repress his feelings as he grew up, leading to outbursts of anger or frustration when he did show them. The focus of Paul's therapeutic process was on acquiring skills for emotional control, such as mindfulness, and exploring the origins of his hidden anger. Therapy for individuals like Paul often focuses on retraining emotional responses and teaching them to acknowledge emotions without judgment. Healing from a narcissistic father's dismissiveness requires the child (now an adult) to reconnect with their emotional self and learn healthier ways to express feelings.

Ajay's Story: The Shame of Never Being "Good Enough"

Ajay's father never expressed satisfaction, causing him to grow up feeling constantly inadequate. No matter what Ajay did, it was never enough. If he got a B on a test, his father would say, "Why not A?" If he won second place in a competition, his father would ask, "Why weren't you first?"

This constant criticism didn't just motivate Ajay to work harder—it filled him with shame, a kind of negative reinforcement.

Ajay's father had a way of making everything. Ajay seemed insignificant. If Ajay were proud of something, his father would tear it down.

"You think that's good? Anyone could do that," his father would say with a dismissive shrug. The message Ajay received was clear: You're not good enough, and you'll never be good enough.

This kind of environment causes children to internalize shame. Ajay didn't just feel bad about his achievements—he felt wrong about who he was.

He grew up believing that something inherently was wrong with him, and no matter how hard he tried, he would always fall short.

In adulthood, this shame followed Ajay everywhere. At work, he struggled to take pride in his accomplishments. Even when his boss praised him, Ajay would brush it off, thinking he didn't deserve this. He was constantly waiting for everyone around him to realize he was ordinary, that he wasn't as good as they thought.

In relationships, Ajay's shame made him distant. He avoided getting too close to people because he feared they would see the real him—who wasn't good enough. He would push people away, fearing rejection before they could reject him. Ajay's fear of failure and deep-seated shame created a barrier that kept him from thoroughly enjoying life.

The fear that binds everything together.

Fear of rejection, failure, and not being loved haunted both Alia and Ajay. This fear didn't just appear in certain situations; it became a constant undercurrent in their lives.

Alia's fear originated from thinking they would leave her unless she constantly pleased everyone. Throughout her childhood, she discovered that her worth depended on her ability to help others.

This belief carried into her adult relationships. She was afraid to set boundaries or ask for what she needed because she thought it might drive people away. If she wasn't constantly giving, would anyone stick around?

The fear that Ajay experienced was subtly different. He feared that no matter what he did, he would fail—and failure, in his mind, meant rejection. Ajay avoided taking risks, even in his career, because the idea of failing was too much for him to handle. His fear wasn't just about messing up a task—it was about proving his father right, about reinforcing the belief that he wasn't good enough.

The way these emotions show up in adulthood.

Guilt, shame, and fear can cause immense harm in adulthood. For Alia, the guilt made her **overextend** herself to the point of burnout. Because of her belief that it was her duty to keep everyone happy, she consistently took on more than she could handle. It made her feel drained, unacknowledged, and sometimes resentful.

Ajay's shame kept him from pursuing his dreams. He had talent and potential, but believing he wasn't good enough held him back. He would sabotage his success by not trying or quitting when things got tough. Unable to overcome his fear of failure, he remained trapped and unable to progress.

Both Alia and Ajay faced challenges in their relationships. Alia's inclination to please others caused her to become a doormat in certain relationships, while Ajay's apprehension of rejection made him emotionally closed off. Despite their longing for connection, their toxic emotions hindered them.

Healing from Guilt, Shame, and Fear

It is possible to recover from toxic emotions, but it necessitates self-reflection and sometimes therapy. Alia eventually grasped the importance of setting boundaries and realizing she wasn't accountable for others' feelings. She prioritized herself and recognized her worth, deserving love and respect for her actions and essence.

On his healing journey, Ajay confronted his shame without hesitation. He had to learn to be proud of his accomplishments and not constantly judge himself based on his father's impossible benchmarks. With time, his self-confidence increased, and he took small actions to follow his passions, learning that failure didn't equate to worthlessness. Fear, guilt, and shame are toxic emotions that can take root in childhood and linger into adulthood, shaping how we see ourselves and how we relate to the world. These emotions deeply affected Alia and Ajay, shaping their identities and influencing their relationships, work, and well-being. But by recognizing these patterns and taking steps toward healing, they reclaimed their sense of self and moved forward.

How Children Deal with Emotional Abuse: Growing Up in Survival Mode.

Children raised in toxic, emotionally abusive environments can't simply experience a carefree childhood. To protect themselves emotionally, they develop coping mechanisms, but these strategies have consequences when carried into adulthood.

For example, Natalia and Sujay, two individuals who grew up in survival mode, each finding different ways to endure emotional abuse in their homes.

Natalia, The Person Who Is Always Striving to Please Everyone

Growing up, Natalia had a mother who could never find satisfaction. Nothing Natalia did was ever good enough. If she got an A on a test, her mother would ask why it wasn't an A+. If Natalia cleaned her room, her mother would find a speck of dust and criticize her. It wasn't just about her performance—her mother would also attack her appearance, telling her things like, "You need to lose weight" or "Why don't you dress better?" From a young age, Natalia learned that the only way to avoid criticism was to do everything she could to keep her mother happy.

Yet, pleasing her mother was always an uphill task. Her mother's mood would fluctuate suddenly, leaving Natalia unsure what to expect. Her mother's behavior was inconsistent; sometimes kind and affectionate, other times cold and distant, or even outright cruel. Natalia transformed herself into the ultimate crowd-pleaser. She was as pleasant as possible to prevent her mother from getting upset. She would suppress her feelings, never arguing or standing up for herself, because confrontation always led to more emotional abuse.

This people-pleasing behavior helped Natalia avoid some of the worst outbursts as a child. She thought that if she could be perfect enough, maybe her mother would finally love her how she wanted. But as Natalia grew older, this coping mechanism became ingrained. During her adulthood, she made a habit of always prioritizing others over herself. Even if it meant staying late and tiring herself out, she would still take on extra tasks at work. Because she feared disappointing her partner or friends, she refrained from expressing her desires and preferences in her relationships. Through her survival mode, Natalia learned to sacrifice herself selflessly in pursuit of peace. But living this way meant losing sight of who she indeed was. She built her identity around bringing happiness to others, which left her feeling drained, unfulfilled, and deeply anxious.

Sujay's Story: The Chameleon

Sujay's parents raised him in a household with an emotionally unpredictable father who had narcissistic tendencies. One minute, his father would be calm and rational; the next, he'd be shouting and throwing things in a rage. Sujay always felt on edge because of the constant uncertainty, like he was tiptoeing on eggshells.

Because he never knew what could trigger his father, he became highly perceptive of his father's emotions and adjusted himself to avoid being targeted.

To survive, Sujay adopted a chameleon-like coping mechanism. The moment he entered a room, he could instantly gauge its emotional atmosphere. Sujay would stay out of sight if his father seemed angry, quietly disappearing into his bedroom.

If his father were in a good mood, Sujay would act cheerful, mirroring his father's emotions to avoid confrontation. He perfected the skill of seamlessly blending in and disappearing when required.

Sujay's adaptability allowed him to endure his unpredictable home. It allowed him to avoid much of his father's wrath by not being noticed. Like Natalia's tendency to please others, Sujay's adaptability continued into adulthood.

He found he would shift his personality depending on who he was around. Sujay would become overly agreeable if his boss were demanding, even if he disagreed internally. In his friendships, he would mold himself to fit others' desires, occasionally faking enjoyment of things he wasn't interested in, preventing conflicts.

Sujay's **identity crisis** stemmed from his ability to change his color based on the circumstances. He had become disconnected from his preferences, opinions, and feelings after spending a significant portion of his life accommodating others. Despite being surrounded by people, he felt disconnected and isolated.

Survival mode affects us in the long run.

Natalia and Sujay's coping mechanisms were crucial for their survival as kids, but as adults, these behaviors turned harmful. They both faced anxiety and self-doubt, constantly doubting themselves due to neglecting their own needs and emotions.

Setting boundaries proved difficult for Natalia, who constantly aimed to please others. Terrified of rejection or conflict, she would never decline, even if it had negative consequences. Her anxiety grew over time because she felt trapped in a cycle of trying to make everyone happy while neglecting herself.

Sujay felt lost in his adult life. **He had adapted so much to other people's expectations that he didn't know what he wanted for himself.** He would follow whatever his boss said in his career, even if it didn't align with his values or interests. Sujay struggled to be vulnerable in his relationships because he kept hiding his true self behind a mask of whatever the other person wanted him to be.

Natalia and Sujay discovered that the coping mechanisms from their childhood hindered their ability to live authentic and fulfilling lives.

Transition out of survival mode.

The first step toward healing is recognizing that you've been living in survival mode. Natalia began therapy and worked on setting boundaries. Initially, this posed a significant challenge for her as it contradicted her upbringing. The fear of being rejected for not constantly saying yes was something she had to confront. Yet, as the days passed, she realized relationships require mutual respect, not endless self-sacrifice. Creating boundaries enabled her to preserve her energy and concentrate on her needs like never before.

Sujay's path to healing involved rediscovering his authentic self. Through therapy, he examined his true identity beyond the personas he adopted for others. He initially started small by making decisions that reflected his preferences, such as choosing the restaurant for dinner or what food to eat, rather than constantly yielding to others' wishes. Gradually, he started reconstructing his identity, mastering the art of expressing himself openly and without fear of judgment or disagreement.

Natalia and Sujay had to abandon their old coping mechanisms that no longer served them. The process of healing from a survival mindset isn't immediate; it entails reestablishing self-trust and understanding that living in perpetual fear of rejection, conflict, or emotional abuse is unnecessary.

Coping mechanisms develop in children from emotionally abusive environments to survive. Natalia started prioritizing others' happiness and sacrificing her needs, while Sujay adapted to different roles like a chameleon to avoid conflict. These tactics enabled them to endure their troubled upbringings, yet in adulthood, they experienced feelings of being lost and anxious.

Breaking free from these survival patterns takes self-reflection, patience, and often professional guidance. Natalia discovered the importance of setting boundaries and prioritizing her well-being, while Sujay found his identity again by making choices aligned with his desires. Letting go of old coping mechanisms and embracing self-respect, authenticity, and emotional freedom allows for moving beyond survival mode.

Chapter 3: The Lingering Scars of Childhood

"Fathers should know that sons follow their example, not advice." – Unknown.

Subunits:

- The influence of narcissistic abuse on relationships in adulthood
- The Invisible Wounds: Self-Esteem, Anxiety, and Depression
- Attracting Narcissistic Life Partners

The Influence of Narcissistic Abuse on Relationships in Adulthood

Narcissistic abuse leaves lasting marks on how we see ourselves and interact with others, especially in our adult relationships. It can shape how we choose partners, feel, and behave in relationships. **People who've experienced narcissistic abuse may find themselves repeatedly drawn to toxic partners or caught in cycles of co-dependency.** Let us explore this with the help of two cases of Joe and Hera—to understand how these patterns can repeat in real life.

Joe's Story: The Trap of Co-Dependency

Joe grew up with a father who constantly criticized him. No matter what Joe did, it was never enough. His father would tell him things like, "You're lazy," "You'll never succeed," or "Why can't you be more like your brother?" Over time, Joe internalized these messages. He started believing he wasn't worthy of love or approval unless he worked hard to earn it. This kind of upbringing shaped his view of relationships. He became what we call co-dependent.

In adulthood, Joe was drawn to people who reminded him of his father—emotionally unavailable, critical, and dismissive.

He met Laura, a woman who seemed exciting at first. She was charismatic, full of life, and very confident. But soon, the red flags started to show. Laura would often put Joe down in small ways. She'd say things like, "You're so sensitive," or "Why can't you ever just relax?" She expected him to always be there for her, but when Joe needed emotional support, she would dismiss his feelings, saying things like, "Oh, stop being so dramatic."

Despite this, Joe stayed in the relationship. Why? Because deep down, he felt he needed to **"earn" her love.** He believed that if he tried harder and was more patient or attentive, Laura would eventually love and appreciate him. But that never happened. The more Joe gave, the more Laura took. **And the more Laura took, the more empty Joe felt**. Joe realized he was trapped in a cycle of trying to please someone who would never be satisfied.

Joe's relationship with Laura mirrored the one he had with his father. He connected his self-worth with someone else's approval. He was willing to sacrifice his needs and happiness to feel loved, even by someone who treated him poorly. Joe's co-dependency kept him trapped in a toxic relationship for years until he finally realized that love shouldn't be something you have to work for constantly. Love should flow freely between people, not something you must continually work for.

Case Study: The Over-Responsible Child

By Cermak and Brown (1982)

Narcissistic Fathers and the Development of Codependency

Another consequence of having narcissistic fathers is the emergence of codependency in their children. In their research, Cermak and Brown (1982) showed how offspring of narcissistic fathers may neglect their own needs in favor of others' needs as a result of being taught to prioritize their father's needs.

"Sarah," now in her 40s, grew up with a father who constantly demanded attention and admiration. Sarah was regularly tasked with tending to his emotional needs, leaving her little room to address her own feelings.

As a grown-up, Sarah frequently ended up in relationships where she assumed the role of caregiver, placing her partner's needs before hers. Feeling exhausted and resentful, she turned to therapy for help.

During therapy, Sarah focused on identifying her codependent tendencies and realizing how her father's narcissistic expectations influenced her actions.

She grasped the concept of establishing boundaries and putting her needs first, understanding that it was acceptable to decline without feeling guilty.

Healing from codependency requires mastering the art of setting positive emotional and relational boundaries. Therapy focuses on empowering individuals to rediscover their needs and engage in self-care without fearing being seen as selfish.

******

Hera's Story: The Craving of Toxic Attractions

Hera grew up with a narcissistic mother who always needed to be the center of attention and demanded constant admiration. Hera's mother would get angry, give her the silent treatment, or use guilt trips if she didn't receive the praise she desired from her daughter. Hera learned early on that her needs didn't matter. Her role was to care for her mother's emotions, even if it meant sacrificing her own. Her father was a passive observer and often supported his wife.

As Hera got older, she began attracting partners with traits similar to her mother's. Subconsciously, Hera was attracted to charming, confident men with a larger-than-life personality. She liked they were confident and seemed to know what they wanted. But beneath the surface, these men were **controlling and manipulative**, just like her mother had been.

When Hera met Daniel, she fell for him instantly. He was intelligent, successful, and charming. He made her feel special, at least in the beginning. But after a few months, his controlling side began to show. He questioned her about where she was going, who she was talking to, and even what she wore. He didn't like it when she spent time with friends and would say, **"Why do you need to hang out with them when you have me?"**

At first, Hera thought he was just being protective, but over time, she realized Daniel was trying to isolate her.

Like her mother, Daniel would lash out if Hera didn't do things his way. If she tried to assert herself or voice her opinion, Daniel would turn the tables on her, making her feel guilty for "causing problems" in the relationship. He made her doubt herself, constantly saying things like, "You're overreacting" or "You're too sensitive."

But the scariest part was Hera couldn't walk away. She felt trapped, even though she knew the relationship was toxic. There was something familiar about Daniel's behavior, and in a twisted way, it felt "normal" to her.

Hera found herself caught in a cycle of toxic attraction. She kept getting involved with men who were emotionally abusive because that's what she knew. Her mother's treatment of her had conditioned Hera to believe that love was supposed to be difficult and painful. It wasn't until Hera came to counseling therapy that she understood this pattern. It helped her see that her relationship with Daniel reflected her unresolved issues with her mother.

She had never learned how to set boundaries or prioritize her needs, so she kept finding herself in relationships where her needs didn't matter.

The Common Thread

Both Joe and Hera's stories show how narcissistic abuse during childhood can shape adult relationships. Joe's co-dependency made him feel like he had to earn love by giving more of himself than was healthy.

Hera's toxic attractions led her to seek out partners who mirrored her mother's controlling and manipulative behavior.

In both cases, the abuse they experienced in their early years set the stage for how they would interact with others in adulthood.

Narcissistic abusers make people believe that their worth is dependent on someone else's approval or admiration. They may become overly dependent on their partners, like Joe, or attracted to toxic, selfish individuals like Hera. These patterns can be hard to break because they're often rooted in deep-seated beliefs about self-worth and love.

Breaking the Cycle

So, how can someone like Joe or Hera break from these patterns? It starts with recognizing the role that early abuse played in shaping their current relationship dynamics. The connection between past and present is better understood through counseling and self-reflection.

Learning that love doesn't have to be earned was crucial for Joe. He had to understand that successful relationships require mutual respect and support, not constant sacrifice. Joe also needed to work on his self-esteem and know that he was worthy of love, just as he was, without having to prove anything.

For Hera, breaking the cycle of toxic attractions meant learning to set boundaries. She had to understand that she didn't have to tolerate controlling or abusive behavior, no matter how charming or confident the other person seemed. Therapy helped her develop a sense of self-worth that wasn't tied to her partner's approval.

Conclusion

Narcissistic abuse can leave deep scars, but it doesn't have to define someone's future relationships. By recognizing the patterns stemming from past experiences, people like Joe and Hera can break free from toxic dynamics and build healthier, more fulfilling connections. It takes time, self-awareness, and often professional help, but healing is possible.

The Invisible Wounds: Self-Esteem, Anxiety, and Depression

The psychological effects of narcissistic abuse can stay with someone long after the abuse ends, leaving invisible wounds that can severely affect mental health.

These wounds often show up as low self-esteem, anxiety, and depression. People who have gone through this kind of emotional trauma might find it hard to feel good about themselves, struggle with constant worry, or slip into depression when life doesn't go the way they hope.

Let me share the stories of three individuals—Nisha, Kia, and Vivan—each dealing with different aspects of these long-term mental health struggles to show how deeply these invisible wounds can affect someone's life.

Nisha's Story: Struggling to Find Herself

Nisha is 40 years old, and despite her age, she still feels lost regarding her identity. Growing up, Nisha's mother was a classic narcissist. Her mother dictated how Nisha should dress, behave, and even think.

If Nisha tried to express a different opinion or do something independently, her mother would rebuke her. "You're going to embarrass me," her mother would say. Or, "You don't know what's best for you; I do." Over time, Nisha started believing that her mother's opinion was more important than hers. She didn't trust herself to make decisions.

Now, as an adult, Nisha still carries this burden. She struggles to figure out who she is, what she wants, and what makes her happy. Every decision feels like a monumental task. Should she switch jobs? Is she good enough to pursue the hobby she loves—painting? Or should she continue following the " safe " and "right path?"

Nisha finds herself constantly doubting her abilities and her choices. This lack of confidence comes from years of being told she wasn't good enough or smart enough to make her own decisions. **Her self-esteem is so low that even**

when she succeeds, she doubts whether it's truly because of her skills or luck.

The invisible wound here is a deep sense of self-doubt, and it's been years in the making. Nisha's struggle is not just about figuring out her career or hobbies; it's about reclaiming the ability to trust herself. Nisha's mother constantly controlled her, leaving her feeling like she wasn't allowed to have an identity of her own, and she still struggles to overcome this feeling.

Kia's Story: Living with Anxiety and Insomnia

Kia is 30 years old and has been dealing with anxiety for most of her life. It started when she was a child, living with a father who was unpredictable and quick to anger. One minute, he would be calm; the next, he would lash out over something as small as a spilled glass of water. Kia learned to walk on eggshells around him, constantly scanning for signs of his mood shifts. She became hypervigilant, always ready to apologize, always trying to avoid triggering his rage.

As an adult, this anxiety followed her. Instead of worrying about her father's anger, she worries about everything—her job, relationships, and future. Kia has developed insomnia and is unable to shut off her mind at night. The minute she sleeps, her thoughts race: "What if I get fired?" "What if my partner leaves me?" "What if something terrible happens tomorrow?"

Kia came to me for help with her anxiety disorder and insomnia, desperate for some relief. She had tried everything—meditation, exercise, even medication—but nothing seemed to calm the constant stream of worry. The problem, of course, goes deeper than just sleepless nights.

Kia's anxiety is rooted in her past experiences with her father's emotional abuse. When you spend your childhood in constant fear, it rewires your brain always to expect the worst. **Her mind never learned how to relax because it was always on high alert, ready for the next outburst.**

Kia's anxiety is an invisible wound that makes her feel unsafe in her own life. Even when everything seems to go well, she can't shake the feeling that disaster is approaching. Such is the long-term impact of growing up in an environment where you never knew when the next emotional blow would come.

Vivan's Story: The Battle with Depression and Approval

Vivan is 35 years old and works as a software engineer. He's good at his job, but he struggles intensely with depression whenever his efforts go unrecognized. Vivan's need for approval comes from his childhood, where his parents praised him only when he accomplished something that made them look good. His parents ignored or criticized him if he didn't meet their high standards. "We expect more from you," his father would say when Vivan's grades weren't perfect. His mother says, "You must work harder to make us proud." This conditional love made Vivan feel like he had to earn his worth. As an adult, he craves external validation to feel good about himself. If his boss or colleagues don't acknowledge his hard work, he sinks into a deep depression.

He believes he's a failure, even when doing a great job. His self-worth depends entirely on how others perceive him, and if that perception is negative—or even neutral—he spirals into self-doubt and sadness. When Vivan doesn't receive praise for his work, his parents' past criticism makes him feel inadequate. The depression hits hard because, in his mind, failing to meet expectations is the same as being unworthy of love or respect. This invisible wound—the belief that his worth depends on others' approval—fuels a cycle of highs and lows that he struggles to escape.

The Long-Term Psychological Impact

These three stories—Nisha's struggle with identity, Kia's battle with anxiety, and Vivan's fight against depression— illustrate the long-term effects of narcissistic abuse. Early experiences of emotional abuse, manipulation, and neglect caused the invisible wounds that Nisha, Kia, and Vivan carry.

Their childhood treatment deeply influences the pain they feel in their adulthood.

Narcissistic parents often shape their children's view of themselves in damaging ways. When a parent is hypercritical, controlling, or emotionally unavailable, it can lead to issues like low self-esteem, anxiety, and depression that follow a person into adulthood. These wounds are invisible because they don't leave physical scars but cut just as deeply. The constant need for approval, the inability to trust oneself, or the sense of never feeling safe can make life incredibly difficult to navigate.

Healing the Wounds

Recovering from these invisible wounds takes time, self-awareness, and often professional help. In such cases, therapy is helpful for people like Nisha, Kia, and Vivan to recognize the connection between their current struggles and their past experiences. For Nisha, the journey is about reclaiming her sense of self and learning to trust her voice.

Kia's healing will involve finding ways to calm her anxiety and feel safe in her own life. Vivan must learn that his worth isn't dependent on external validation and that he can find value within himself, regardless of how others see him.

While the wounds from narcissistic abuse can feel permanent, healing is possible. It requires self-compassion, patience, acceptance, and the willingness to confront the painful memories of the past.

But with time and support, it's possible to break free from the patterns that keep these invisible wounds alive and to live a life where the approval or actions of others no longer determine self-worth, peace, and joy.

Attracting Narcissistic Life Partners

Attracting narcissistic partners may feel like a cruel twist of fate for those who grew up in narcissistic households. You would think that, having lived through such emotional abuse, they would steer clear of similar relationships.

Often, survivors of narcissistic abuse are attracted to people who share the same toxic traits as their parents without realizing it. Why?

Because it feels familiar, like coming home, let me share the stories of Diya, Sia, and Herman—three people struggling with this very pattern. Narcissistic parents raised all three, and now, as adults, they find themselves in relationships that mirror those unhealthy dynamics. They are at a breaking point, wondering if they should stay or leave.

Diya's Story: The Golden Child Trap

Diya grew up with a grandiose narcissistic mother who treated her as the golden child. Her mother praised Diya endlessly, not for who she truly was, but for how she made her mother look. "You're so special," her mother would say, "You're the only one who understands me." Diya's mother constantly reinforced the idea that she was superior to others. If Diya ever stepped out of line or failed to meet her mother's high expectations, the praise quickly turned into criticism. This back-and-forth left her constantly seeking approval, striving to remain in her mother's good graces.

As an adult, Diya found herself in a relationship with Raj, a man who seemed charming, successful, and confident—everything she thought she wanted. But over time, Raj showed his selfish side. He would shower her with compliments one minute, and the next, he would criticize her for not living up to his impossible standards. It was a cycle that felt eerily similar to her relationship with her mother.

At first, Diya didn't see the pattern. Raj's praise made her feel valued and unique, just like her mother's had. But as his control and criticism escalated, Diya started questioning why she was always trying to please him. It felt familiar, yes—but familiar in a suffocating way.

Now, Diya is at a crossroads. She realizes that staying with Raj means living in a state of constant validation-seeking, just as she did with her mother. But breaking free feels terrifying. After all, who is she without someone telling her how special she is? Diya has begun to understand that what she thought was love was a need for validation—a dangerous game that keeps her trapped in unhealthy relationships.

Sia's Story: The Emotional Roller Coaster

Sia's mother was a **covert** narcissist, which meant the abuse wasn't as blatant. Instead of grand gestures and loud boasts, Sia's mother used guilt, manipulation, and emotional games to keep control. One minute, she would act like the perfect mother, caring and concerned. The next, she would pull the rug out from under Sia, making her feel worthless and unloved. Sia never knew what to expect, which kept her on edge, constantly trying to win her mother's love and approval.

As an adult, Sia ended up in a relationship with Ethan, a man who initially seemed kind and attentive. But soon enough, she noticed the emotional roller coasters starting again. One day, Ethan would act like the perfect boyfriend, buying her gifts, planning romantic dates, and saying everything right.

But the next day, he would criticize or give her the silent treatment without any explanation. Sia felt like she was back in her childhood home, trying to figure out how to keep the peace and win back his affection.

Sia is now at a point where she knows this relationship isn't healthy. She feels drained, anxious, and unsure of herself. But there's also a part of her that's hesitant to leave.

The ups and downs, while painful, are what she's used to. It feels like "normal" love to her. Leaving would mean stepping into the unknown, and that's scary. Sia knows she deserves better, but part of her is still clinging to the hope that she can fix things, that if she tries a little harder, Ethan will change. It's a hope she clung to with her mother that never materialized.

Herman's Story: The Uncaring Father, The Uncaring Partner

Herman's father was a malignant narcissist—a man who took pleasure in control, manipulation, and emotional cruelty. He never cared for Herman in the way a father should. He enjoyed watching Herman fail, only to swoop in with criticism and harsh judgments. "You're not good enough," his father would say. "You'll never amount to anything." Herman grew up believing he was worthless and that no matter how hard he tried, he would never earn his father's love or approval.

Fast forward to adulthood, and Herman found himself in a relationship with Claire, a woman who, on the surface, seemed independent and strong. However, as the relationship progressed, Claire began to display traits that reminded Herman of his father. She was cold, dismissive, and often belittled him when he expressed his feelings. If Herman tried to talk about something that upset him, she would shut him down or make him feel he was overreacting. Just like with his father, Herman felt like no matter what he did, he wasn't good enough for Claire.

Now, Herman is stuck. Part of him knows this relationship is toxic, but another part feels like it's what he deserves. Herman's father conditioned him to believe his son was unworthy of love and affection, and now he's found a partner who reinforces that belief. Breaking free means confronting the idea that he's not inherently flawed—that he deserves a partner who treats him with kindness and respect. But after years of internalizing his father's abuse, Herman struggles to believe that's possible.

Why Do They Stay?

So why do Diya, Sia, and Herman stay in these toxic relationships? The answer is complex, but it often boils down to one thing: familiarity.

When you grow up in a narcissistic household, the chaos and emotional manipulation become your baseline for what relationships should look like. It feels like home. For Diya, the praise and criticism from Raj echo her mother's treatment. For Sia, the emotional roller coasters with Ethan mirror the instability she felt with her mother. For Herman, Claire's coldness and cruelty feel like a continuation of his father's neglect.

The truth is that narcissistic partners often seem attractive to survivors because they trigger the same emotional responses they experienced in childhood. It's a subconscious pull. If you've been conditioned to believe that love means earning approval or enduring emotional abuse, you find those patterns comforting, even though they're harmful.

The Breaking Point

Each of these individuals—Diya, Sia, and Herman—is now standing on the threshold of a decision. Do they stay in these toxic relationships and continue to live out the patterns they've known their entire lives? Or do they break free and risk stepping into the unknown? It's not an easy choice.

For Diya, the challenge is learning to value herself without needing external validation. She sees that Raj's approval isn't the same as love, but letting go of that need is terrifying.

Sia is realizing that the emotional highs and lows she's been living with aren't a sign of passion or deep connection— they're a symptom of emotional abuse. She's scared to leave but knows that staying will only bring more pain.

Herman faces the most demanding challenge: believing he's worthy of love and care. His father's voice is still in his head, telling him he's not good enough, and Claire's behavior only reinforces that belief. But deep down, he's starting to understand that this isn't true.

Break that Cycle

Breaking the cycle of attracting narcissistic partners takes time and self-awareness. Diya, Sia, and Herman are all at a point where they can see the patterns, and that's the first step.

Understanding that the familiarity of these relationships isn't love but emotional conditioning can help them heal.

Therapy, self-reflection, and building a support system are crucial. It's about learning to recognize red flags early on and understanding that healthy relationships don't involve manipulation, emotional abuse, or constant validation-seeking. For each of them, the path to healing involves redefining what love looks like and finding peace in relationships built on mutual respect, care, and genuine affection—not on control, manipulation, or fear.

And while breaking free from these patterns is hard, it's possible. They all have the opportunity to create a future where they're attracted to people who care for them, not those who cause them pain. It's about creating a new "home"—one that's filled with love, kindness, and emotional safety.

Chapter 4: Breaking the Cycle

"You survived the abuse. You are going to survive the recovery"-Unknown

- **Recognizing the Abuse**

- **Setting Boundaries with a Narcissistic Parent**

- **Healing the Inner Child**

Recognizing the Abuse

Recognizing and acknowledging narcissistic abuse can be one of the most challenging steps for those who grew up with narcissistic parents. It's not common knowledge that the way people were treated was unusual. They may have internalized the blame, thinking they were the problem. It's complicated because narcissistic parents often weave a confusing mix of love, manipulation, and control, making it hard to identify the abuse.

Joe and Hera, like many others, spent most of their lives not recognizing that their parents were abusing them. Their stories underscore the ease with which one can remain trapped in that cycle and the importance of finally acknowledging what is truly happening.

Joe's Story: The Pressure of Perfection

Joe grew up with a father who demanded perfection in everything. Joe's father insisted that he excel at school, sports, and every hobby he pursued as a child. If he ever fell short, even by a little, his father would scold him harshly, making him feel worthless. Joe remembers his father saying things like, "You're better than this," or "I don't understand why you can't do better." But whenever Joe succeeded, his father would downplay it. "Anyone could have done that," he would say, "Don't get too proud of yourself."

For years, Joe didn't see this as abuse. He thought it was tough love— his father wanted the best for him. It wasn't until Joe reached his 30s that he realized something was wrong. He constantly strived for perfection in his career, feeling like nothing he did was ever good enough. He was exhausted, stressed, and unhappy but didn't know why.

In counseling sessions, Joe started unpacking his childhood. He began to see that his father's constant criticism wasn't just tough love; it was emotional abuse. His father's impossible standards and lack of praise weren't motivating Joe—they were breaking him down. Joe had spent all his time trying to win his father's approval, but the truth was, he never could.

His father used praise and criticism to control him, ensuring Joe always felt like he wasn't good enough.

Realizing this was painful. Joe always believed that his father loved him and wanted him to succeed. Acknowledging the abuse meant admitting that his father's treatment wasn't about love at all—it was about **power and control.** Joe felt conflicted, even angry, as he worked through these feelings. But recognizing the abuse was the first step towards healing. Joe started setting boundaries with his father and stopped seeking his approval. It wasn't easy, but Joe began to reclaim his sense of self-worth, realizing that he was enough, just as he was.

Hera's Story: The Emotional Manipulation

Hera's mother was a different kind of narcissist. She didn't demand perfection, but she controlled Hera through emotional manipulation. Hera's mother always made her feel guilty for not being the perfect daughter. Her mother would say things like, "After all I've done for you, this is how you repay me?" or "You're so ungrateful; no one will ever love you as I do."

Hera was constantly walking on tenterhooks, trying to avoid upsetting her mother. Even as an adult, she found herself putting her mother's needs first, often at the expense of her own well-being. Hera profoundly felt her mother's love and saw maintaining peace as her duty. She didn't realize that this dynamic was toxic. It wasn't until she started noticing how drained and anxious she felt after interacting with her mother that she began to question what was happening.

One day, after a particularly heated argument, Hera confided in a close friend. Her friend asks, "Do you ever feel like your mom is manipulating you?" That question hit Hera hard. She had never thought of it that way. She always believed that her mother's behavior was part of their complicated relationship.

But as she reflected, Hera realized that her mother's love always came with strings attached.

Her mother would guilt-trip Hera and give her the silent treatment if she didn't do what she wanted. It wasn't love—it was control.

Hera started reading about narcissistic abuse and realized her mother fit the description perfectly. She felt a mix of relief and devastation. On one hand, she finally had an explanation for why she always felt so drained and anxious around her mother. On the other hand, it hurt to admit that her mother's love wasn't unconditional. Hera had spent her life believing that her mother's approval was the key to her happiness, but now she saw that this approval came at a high price—her own sense of self.

The Difficulty of Recognition

For both Joe and Hera, recognizing the abuse took time. Narcissistic parents are often skilled at disguising their behavior as love or care, which makes it difficult for their children to see the truth. Joe's father instilled in him the belief that only perfection would earn him love, while Hera's mother taught her that love required guilt and obligation.

One of the reasons it's so hard to recognize narcissistic abuse is that it doesn't always look like traditional abuse. There's no physical violence, and the emotional manipulation can be subtle. Joe and Hera both grew up feeling confused, thinking they might be the problem. Joe thought he wasn't good enough, and Hera thought she wasn't grateful enough. They internalized their parents' messages, which kept them trapped in the cycle of abuse.

But once they started recognizing the patterns, everything became more evident. Joe saw that his father's expectations were impossible and that his constant criticism was a way to control him. Hera realized that her mother's emotional manipulation was not love but a tactic to keep her dependent and obedient. Recognizing the abuse allowed them both to take the first steps toward healing.

Validation and Acknowledgment

One of the most essential parts of healing from narcissistic abuse is validating your own experience. Joe and Hera both struggled with this. Joe struggled to acknowledge his father's abuse because he was raised believing his father's actions were meant to help him succeed. Hera felt guilty for questioning if her mother was abusive, because she had been conditioned to believe that her mother's love was all she needed.

But validation is crucial. It's about acknowledging that the pain you've experienced is real and that you didn't deserve it. Joe had to accept that his father's harsh criticism wasn't about making him a better person but about control. Hera had to come to terms with the fact that her mother's guilt trips weren't about love—they were about manipulation.

By recognizing and acknowledging the abuse, Joe and Hera began to reclaim their sense of self. They no longer felt the need to seek their parents' approval or bend to their emotional manipulation. They started setting boundaries and focusing on their own emotional well-being instead of constantly trying to please their narcissistic parents.

Moving Forward

For those who grew up with narcissistic parents, identifying and understanding the abuse is the first step toward healing. It's not easy, and it often comes with a lot of emotional pain. But once you see the abuse for what it is, you can start to rebuild your sense of self-worth and break free from the toxic patterns that have kept you trapped.

Joe and Hera are still working through their feelings, but they've made progress. Joe is learning to let go of the need for his father's approval, and Hera is setting boundaries with her mother for the first time in her life. They've both started to realize that they are enough just as they are—that they don't need to prove their worth to anyone, especially not to their narcissistic parents. Recognizing and acknowledging the abuse is hard, but it's also liberating. It's the first step toward a healthier, happier life—one where you're free from the emotional chains of narcissistic abuse.

Setting Boundaries with a Narcissistic Parent

Setting boundaries with a narcissistic parent is one of the most critical steps to protect yourself from further emotional harm. It can be tricky, even painful because narcissistic parents rarely respect boundaries and will push back hard when you try to set them. But it's essential for your well-being.

Let's talk about how Nisha, Kia, and Vivan, who grew up with narcissistic parents, each learned to set boundaries and protect themselves. Their stories show that while it's not easy, it's possible to reclaim your emotional space and begin to heal.

Nisha's Story: Finding Her Own Voice

Nisha, now 40, spent her entire life feeling like she was living for her mother. Her mother, a strong, controlling figure, always made Nisha feel her own needs didn't matter. Growing up, Nisha was constantly accused of being selfish whenever she tried to articulate her wishes or viewpoints. Her mother would say, "I've sacrificed everything for you, and this is how you repay me?" As an adult, Nisha still felt trapped by this dynamic. Even when she tried to make decisions about her life, like changing careers or moving to a new city, her mother's opinions always loomed over her.

One day, Nisha reached a breaking point.

She was exhausted from constantly putting her mother's needs first and feeling guilty whenever she did something for herself. She decided she needed to set some boundaries. At first, it felt impossible. Every time she tried to say "no" to her mother or assert her own needs, her mother would guilt-trip her, using emotional manipulation to make Nisha feel like a bad daughter.

With the help of therapy, Nisha learned to set boundaries step by step. She started small, saying "no" to things that weren't too emotionally charged, like refusing to run an errand her mother could easily do herself. At first, her mother was furious, accusing Nisha of being selfish. But

Nisha stuck to her boundary, reminding herself she wasn't responsible for her mother's emotions.

As time went on, Nisha grew more confident in setting boundaries. She stopped answering her mother's phone calls at night and no longer allowed her mother to criticize her life choices.

Whenever her mother would start in on her with the usual guilt trips, Nisha would calmly say, "Mom, I will not talk about this with you anymore," and then walk away from the conversation. Her mother still tried to push back, but Nisha stood firm. Over time, her mother's outbursts had lessened, and Nisha finally felt some emotional freedom.

Kia's Story: Protecting Her Mental Health

Kia, 30, had been dealing with severe anxiety and insomnia for years. She often woke up in the middle of the night, her mind racing with worry, replaying conversations with her narcissistic mother. Her mother had always been the center of Kia's world, demanding constant attention and emotional support while giving little in return. Kia felt like she was anxious around her mother, always worried about triggering an emotional outburst.

After years of anxiety, Kia sought professional help and was diagnosed with anxiety. Her therapist helped her recognize that much of her anxiety stemmed from her mother's behavior. Kia realized she had been absorbing her mother's emotional abuse for years, and it was taking a toll on her mental health.

Kia knew she needed to create some distance from her mother, but it felt terrifying. Every time she thought about setting boundaries, she imagined her mother's reaction—tears, anger, or threats to cut her out of her life. But Kia's anxiety had reached a point where she couldn't continue without making a change.

Her first step was to create physical space. As an adult, she reduced the frequency of her visits to her mother's house and stopped answering every phone call immediately.

This simple change gave Kia some breathing room and helped her feel more in control of her own life.

Next, Kia began setting emotional boundaries. Her mother had a habit of dumping all her problems on Kia, treating her like a therapist.

Whenever Kia tried to talk about her own struggles, her mother would change the subject or minimize her feelings. So Kia stopped engaging in those conversations. When her mother vented or unloaded, Kia gently but firmly said, "Mom, I can't talk about this right now. I need to focus on my own mental health." It wasn't easy—her mother reacted with anger and tried to make her feel guilty—but Kia knew that protecting her mental health was more important than appeasing her mother.

Over time, Kia's anxiety began to improve. Setting boundaries didn't fix everything but gave her the space she needed to heal. She still has difficult moments with her mother, but she's learned to prioritize her own well-being, something she never thought she could do.

Vivan's Story: Boundaries in the Workplace and at Home

Vivan, 35, struggled with depression, especially when he felt unappreciated at work or in his relationships. Growing up, his narcissistic parents never showed any interest in Vivan's achievements. If Vivan got a good grade in school, his father would say, "That's expected," and if he didn't do well, he'd get condemned. Her mother would endorse his father most of the times.This constant lack of validation made Vivan crave approval from others, especially his bosses and romantic partners.

As an adult, Vivan found himself in toxic work environments where he worked tirelessly but never felt appreciated. At home, his relationships followed the same pattern—he was always the one giving, while his partners took him for granted. This left Vivan feeling drained and depressed.

After one particularly rough period where his work went unacknowledged and his partner seemed indifferent to his feelings, Vivan reached out to a therapist. Through therapy, he realized that his childhood experiences with his narcissistic father had set the stage for these patterns. He had never learned to set boundaries because he always chased validation.

The first boundary Vivan set was at work. He stopped volunteering for extra projects that went unnoticed and refused to stay late unless absolutely necessary. When his boss didn't appreciate his efforts, Vivan reminded himself that he didn't need external validation to feel worthy. It was hard at first—Vivan had spent years attaching his self-worth to what others thought of him—but slowly, he began to feel more in control of his work life.

In his personal relationships, Vivan also started setting boundaries. He had always been the one to bend over backward for his partner, but now he started asking for what he needed. When his partner ignored his feelings or dismissed his emotions, Vivan calmly said, "I need to feel heard in this relationship. If that's not possible, we need to rethink things." This was a massive step for him because it meant putting his own needs first, something he had never done before.

His partner didn't take the boundary-setting well initially, but Vivan stood his ground. Eventually, his partner began to respect his needs more, and Vivan's depression lifted. He no longer felt so weighed down by the need to please everyone else.

The Importance of Boundaries

Setting boundaries wasn't easy for Nisha, Kia, and Vivan, but it was essential for their emotional well-being. Narcissistic parents don't respect boundaries, so they had to be firm and consistent, even when their parents pushed back. Setting boundaries didn't mean they stopped caring about their parents—it just meant they started caring about themselves, too.

Nisha learned to find her voice and make decisions without guilt. Kia prioritized her mental health over her mother's emotional needs. Vivan stopped chasing validation from others and started valuing himself. Each of them faced challenges along the way, but by setting boundaries, they took control of their own lives and began to heal from the emotional damage caused by their narcissistic parents.

Setting boundaries with a narcissistic parent can feel overwhelming, but it's one of the most important steps in reclaiming your emotional space. It's about protecting yourself from further harm and finally giving yourself the care and respect you deserve. While your parents may never fully respect your boundaries, what matters most is what you do.

Healing the Inner Child

Healing the inner child is about reconnecting with that vulnerable, often wounded part of ourselves that got lost in the chaos of a narcissistic parent's world. When you've grown up with a narcissistic parent, your inner child gets buried under layers of pain, neglect, and confusion. It takes time, self-compassion, and conscious effort to uncover that child and give them the love and care they always needed. Let's look at how Diya, Sia, and Herman each found their paths to healing their younger selves.

Diya's Journey: From the Golden Child to Finding Herself

Diya grew up as the "golden child" of her mother, a grandiose narcissist. On the surface, it looked like Diya had everything. Her mother showered her with praise and attention, but there was always an unspoken condition attached: Diya had to live up to her mother's expectations in every way. Anything less was a betrayal. As a child, Diya learned that her worth came from how well she reflected her mother's ideal image. She was never allowed to have her own identity.

In adulthood, Diya felt lost. Her focus in life was trying to be the perfect daughter, but now, as an adult, she didn't know who she really was. She came to therapy because she felt an emptiness she couldn't explain. The problem? She had lost touch with her inner child, the part of her that had been denied the freedom to explore, make mistakes, and just be a kid by her parents.

To reconnect with her inner child, Diya had first to acknowledge that she wasn't responsible for her mother's approval. Her self-worth was not dependent on her achievements or how well she pleased others. In therapy, Diya started journaling about her childhood, allowing herself to feel the emotions she had buried for so long—confusion, fear, sadness. She wrote letters to her younger self, telling her it was okay to be imperfect, to have needs, and to make mistakes.

At first, it was incredibly painful for Diya to face the reality that her mother's love had been conditional. But slowly, she began to understand that her younger self deserved love and acceptance just for being herself. She started doing things that made her inner child happy, like painting, something she had always loved as a child but was discouraged from doing because it didn't fit her mother's idea of success. This simple act of creativity helped Diya reconnect with that playful, curious part of herself.

As she continued her healing process, Diya realized that her inner child wasn't looking for perfection. She was looking for love, acceptance, and the freedom to just be. Diya finally started to give that to herself.

Sia's Story: Healing from The Emotional Roller Coaster

Sia grew up with a covertly narcissistic mother who constantly took her on emotional rollercoasters. One moment, her mother would be loving and affectionate, and the next, she'd be cold and dismissive. As a child, Sia never knew what to expect, so she learned to constantly monitor her mother's moods and adjust her behavior accordingly to avoid triggering her anger. This hypervigilance left Sia with deep anxiety and a constant fear of abandonment.

As an adult, Sia struggled with relationships. She found herself drawn to emotionally unavailable partners, just like her mother. Every relationship felt like an endless chase for love and approval, leaving her exhausted and empty. She couldn't understand why she kept falling into the same patterns.

During therapy, Sia learned about the concept of inner child from her therapist. Her therapist explained that the part of her that kept chasing unavailable partners was the wounded child who had been chasing her mother's affection for years. The first step in healing her inner child was to acknowledge that this child still lived inside her, desperate for love and validation.

Sia began by reflecting on her childhood. She remembered how scared and lonely she often felt when her mother would withdraw affection without warning. In therapy, she practiced re-parenting her inner child—giving that frightened little girl the love, safety, and validation she never received. Whenever Sia felt anxious or abandoned in her relationships, she would pause and ask herself, "What does my inner child need right now?" Sometimes, it was a simple reminder that she was worthy of love. Other times, she would visualize herself hugging her younger self, offering comfort and reassurance.

One of the most powerful moments in Sia's healing process came when she stopped chasing people who couldn't give her what she needed. She realized that her inner child didn't need to keep reliving the same painful dynamics. By honoring her younger self's needs, Sia began to choose healthier relationships—ones where she was valued and respected.

Sia's inner child, who had spent so many years feeling anxious and neglected, finally found peace knowing that she didn't need to chase anyone's love anymore. She could give herself the love and care she had always longed for.

Herman's Path: Breaking Free from the Malignant Father's Shadow

A malignant, narcissistic father dominated Herman's childhood. His father never cared about Herman's feelings or needs. He actively belittled and bullied Herman, telling him he was worthless and would never amount to anything. As a result, Herman grew up feeling small, invisible, and deeply insecure.

In adulthood, Herman struggled with depression. He found it hard to believe in himself, and even small setbacks would make him feel worthless. His relationships also suffered because he often attracted partners who were just as controlling and dismissive as his father. Herman felt stuck in a cycle of self-doubt and emotional pain.

When Herman started therapy, his therapist introduced the idea of healing his inner child. At first, Herman was skeptical. He didn't think revisiting his childhood would help—after all, what was the point of thinking about the past when his father had already done so much damage? But his therapist encouraged him to look deeper.

Herman began to realize that his inner child was still carrying the wounds of his father's cruelty. That child had learned to believe he was worthless because his father had taught him that way. In therapy, Herman started to reframe those beliefs. He began to challenge the narrative ingrained in him—he wasn't worthless, had value, and deserved to be treated with respect.

To reconnect with his inner child, Herman started doing activities that brought him joy as a kid, things he hadn't allowed himself to enjoy in years. He rediscovered his love for drawing, an activity his father used to mock him. He also began practicing self-compassion, speaking to himself how he wished someone had spoken to him when he was younger.

One of the hardest parts of Herman's healing journey was confronting the anger he had buried for so long. He had always suppressed his anger because he was afraid of becoming like his father—harsh and cruel. But in therapy, he learned that anger wasn't the problem. It was how you processed it. Herman began journaling about his anger, allowing himself to express the pain and frustration that he had suppressed for years. This helped him release some of the emotional baggage weighing him down. Slowly, Herman's depression began to lift. Herman's reconnection with his inner child allowed him to give validation and love that had been denied to that child for so long. And in doing so, Herman finally started to believe in himself again.

The Power of Healing the Inner Child

Reconnecting with their inner children was a transformative experience for Diya, Sia, and Herman. Each of them had been carrying the wounds of their childhood into adulthood, whether it was Diya's struggle with identity, Sia's anxiety and relationship patterns, or Herman's feelings of worthlessness and depression. By acknowledging the pain of their younger selves and giving those inner children the love and care they had always needed, they each found a path to healing.

Healing the inner child doesn't happen overnight. It's a process of learning to re-parent yourself and give yourself the love, safety, and validation you didn't receive as a child. For many survivors of narcissistic parents, this is the key to breaking free from the emotional scars of the past. It allows you to stop seeking approval from others, to select healthier relationships, and to ultimately feel at peace with yourself. If you've grown up with a narcissistic parent, healing your inner child might be one of the most powerful steps you can take in your journey of recovery. It's about permitting yourself to feel, grieve, and heal. Most importantly, it's about reconnecting with that vulnerable part of yourself that deserves all the love and care in the world—something your narcissistic parent could never give you, but you can give to yourself.

Chapter 5: Rebuilding Your Life After Trauma

"Healing doesn't mean the damage never existed. It means the damage no longer controls our lives"-Unknown

Subunits:

- Finding Your Voice to Reclaim Power
- Seeking Healthy Relationships
- The Role of Therapy and Self-Help

Parental Narcissism and its Role in Childhood Trauma

Case Study: PTSD (Post-Traumatic Stress Disorder) in Adult Children of Narcissistic Mothers

A study conducted by Thomas et al. (2019) examined the connection between narcissistic parenting and the development of PTSD symptoms in adult children. The study revealed that children of narcissistic mothers may develop trauma symptoms similar to those of emotional abuse victims due to their controlling and critical behavior.

Daughters and sons raised in this type of atmosphere may find themselves constantly on edge, unsure of when their mother's emotions will change.

A research case study focused on "Emily," a woman in her 30s, who sought therapy for panic attacks and struggles with forming trusting relationships. Emily's mother displayed controlling behavior and emotional manipulation, relying on guilt as a tool to influence outcomes. Emily experienced anxiety and hyper-vigilance while growing up, which manifested as symptoms of Complex PTSD.

Emily underwent therapy that centered on recognizing and addressing her trauma responses, leading to healing and a restoration of trust in herself and others.

Healing Focus

Trauma-focused cognitive-behavioral therapy (CBT) and EMDR (Eye Movement Desensitization and Reprocessing) are effective in addressing the PTSD symptoms caused by narcissistic maternal abuse. It further stresses the value of cultivating emotional security and rediscovering how to have faith in others.

Finding Your Voice to Reclaim Power
Stories of Bina, Reya, and Mike

When you grow up with narcissistic parents, it can leave deep emotional scars that you carry into adulthood. The patterns of control, manipulation, and belittling can make you doubt your worth, even long after leaving the family home.

It can feel like you're constantly trying to prove yourself, seeking approval, or staying stuck in unhealthy relationships because that's all you know. But finding your voice and reclaiming your power is possible.

The stories of Bina, Reya, and Mike show how survivors of narcissistic parenting can rebuild their self-worth and independence step by step.

Bina's Story: Letting Go of the Constant Need for Approval

Bina grew up in a household where nothing she did was ever good enough. Her mother criticized everything—her looks, grades, even her friends. "You could have done better," her mother would say, or "Why don't you ever listen to me?" Bina tried hard to meet her mother's impossible standards, believing that if she worked harder, her mother would finally be proud of her.

But no matter what Bina did, her mother always found a way to tear her down. Even as an adult, Bina couldn't shake that need for her mother's approval. It showed up in her job, her friendships, even her marriage. She became a people-pleaser, constantly bending backward to make others happy while ignoring her needs.

It wasn't until her late 30s that Bina started to see the connection between her childhood and how she lived her adult life. A close friend pointed out how Bina seemed to give so much of herself to others but got very little in return. Bina had always thought that was normal, how relationships worked.

But this conversation opened her eyes to how much her mother's selfish behavior had shaped her.Bina began working with a therapist who specialized in childhood trauma.

The therapist helped her understand that her mother's constant criticism wasn't a reflection of Bina's worth but a way her mother maintained control.

Slowly, Bina learned how to set boundaries with her mother and everyone. Saying "no" became a new skill for her, and it initially felt awkward. But the more she practiced, the more she realized she didn't need anyone's approval to feel good about herself.

Bina's most significant victory came when she stopped seeking validation from her mother. She accepted that her mother might never change, and that was okay.

Bina no longer looked for compliments or approval. She learned to trust herself, and for the first time, she felt free. Reclaiming her power wasn't about becoming someone new—it was about letting go of the idea that she needed her mother's approval to be worthy.

Reya's story: Breaking Free from a Narcissistic Parent's Control

Reya's mother had always been the center of her world. Growing up, Reya's mother instilled in her the importance of putting her needs first, whether running errands, dropping plans with friends, or constantly seeking her mother's advice before making any decision. Her mother made it clear: "You need me. You can't do this on your own." And Reya believed her.

As Reya got older, she realized that her mother wasn't just being overprotective. She was controlling. Anytime Reya tried to assert independence, like applying for a job her mother disapproved of, her mother would guilt-trip her. "After all I've done for you, this is how you repay me?" she'd say, and Reya would feel crushed by the guilt. So, she stayed small, afraid of what would happen if she made her own choices.

Reya didn't understand the full extent of her mother's narcissism until she started dating someone who wasn't her mother's choice. When her mother disapproved, Reya was ready to break off the relationship to avoid the conflict. But something stopped her. Reya realized she had been living her entire life trying to make her mother happy, and it wasn't working. No matter what she did, her mother still found reasons to criticize or control her.

That's when Reya began to think about what she wanted for herself for the first time.

With the help of a support group for adult children of narcissists, Reya began to see how unhealthy her relationship with her mother was. She started setting small boundaries, like not sharing every detail of her life or politely but firmly saying no to some of her mother's requests.

The first time Reya said no, her mother lashed out, but Reya stood her ground. It was terrifying, but she didn't back down.

Over time, Reya became more comfortable asserting herself. She started making decisions without consulting her mother and even moved to a new city for a job that her mother had opposed.

Reya didn't completely cut her mother out of her life, but she redefined their relationship on her terms. She no longer sought her mother's permission to live her own life, so Reya reclaimed her power.

Mike's Story: Rebuilding Confidence After a Childhood of Criticism

Mike's father was the kind of man who demanded perfection. He expected Mike to be the best at everything— school, sports, even hobbies. If Mike didn't perform up to his father's standards, he'd hear it: "Why didn't you try harder?" or "You're just being lazy. Over time, Mike began to believe that his father never thought he was good enough. Even as a child, he felt he always fell short, never meeting his father's expectations.

As an adult, Mike carried this feeling into his work. He became a workaholic, always trying to prove himself, constantly pushing harder and harder. No matter how much praise or recognition he received from others, it was never enough to quiet the voice in his head that said he wasn't doing enough.

The breaking point came when Mike's marriage began to suffer. His wife felt neglected, and Mike realized he had spent so much time trying to prove himself at work that he had ignored the most critical parts of his life. He started therapy to deal with his workaholic tendencies, but as he dug deeper, he realized his issues went back to his childhood. His father's relentless criticism had shaped his entire self-image.

Mike's therapist helped him see that his father's impossible standards were about his father's issues, not Mike's abilities or worth. Mike began challenging the voice that told him he wasn't good enough. He stopped measuring his worth by how much he could achieve or how perfect he could be. Instead, he focused on the relationships and experiences that brought him absolute joy.

Mike learned to set boundaries at work, refusing to take on extra projects to prove himself. He spent more time with his family, realizing that his value didn't come from his accomplishments but from who he was. For Mike, reclaiming his power meant recognizing that he didn't have to live up to anyone's expectations but his own.

These three stories—Bina's need for approval, Reya's battle with control, and Mike's struggle for perfection—show that reclaiming your power is a deeply personal process. Growing up with narcissistic parents often leaves you feeling small, dependent, and unsure of yourself. But by recognizing the patterns, setting boundaries, and learning to trust yourself again, you can find your voice and rebuild your sense of self-worth.

It's not about being perfect or becoming someone new—it's about realizing that you've always had the strength to standalone. You just needed to believe it.

Bina, Reya, and Mike- Seeking Healthy Relationships

Growing up with narcissistic parents can leave you confused about what a healthy relationship looks like. Growing up with a controlling and manipulative parent can make it difficult to trust your own judgment, which can lead to toxic friendships, romantic relationships, or work environments in your adult life. The good news is that you can break free from these patterns. Finding and nurturing healthy relationships is a process, but it's entirely possible. Let's look at how Bina, Reya, and Mike each took steps toward healthier connections.

Bina: From People-Pleaser to Finding Balance

Bina's childhood revolved around making her mother happy. Her mother was critical and demanding, always pointing out Bina's flaws and reminding her how much she "owed" her. As a child, Bina believed she could earn her mother's love and approval if she tried hard enough. But that approval never came.

Instead, Bina grew up constantly seeking validation from others, trying to please everyone around her—friends, bosses, even casual acquaintances.

In her 30s, Bina noticed that her relationships felt one-sided. She would go out of her way to help her friends, but no one was there for her when she needed support. She didn't understand why she kept ending up in these friendships, but deep down, Bina feared people wouldn't like her if she wasn't always giving.

Bina's therapist helped her understand that trying to please others stemmed from her childhood desire to earn her mother's approval. She learned healthy relationships aren't about constantly giving or sacrificing yourself. Instead, healthy relationships require balance, where people value and respect each other's needs.

Bina started practicing small ways to build healthier boundaries. She learned how to say no, even when it felt uncomfortable.

For example, when a friend asked her to help plan a last-minute party, Bina politely declined instead of dropping everything. It was hard initially, and she worried her friend would get angry or cut her off. But surprisingly, nothing terrible happened. Her friend understood, and their relationship didn't change.

As Bina became more comfortable setting boundaries, her relationships shifted. Some people faded away, but she realized they were the ones who had been taking advantage of her generosity.

The friends who stuck around respected her new boundaries and were more willing to give back. Over time, Bina noticed a difference in how she felt around these people. She no longer felt drained or resentful. Instead, her relationships felt mutual—she could give and receive without fear.

Bina learned from her experience that genuine relationships don't form by constantly sacrificing oneself to please others. They come from finding a balance where people feel seen, heard, and valued. It took time, but once she started setting boundaries and being true to herself, she attracted people who genuinely respected and cared for her.

Reya: Escaping the Grip of Control

Reya's relationship with her mother was all about control. Her mother dictated every aspect of Reya's life, from her career choices to what she wore. As a child, Reya believed her mother was trying to protect her. But as she grew older, it became clear that her mother's control was suffocating. Reya's mother prevented her from making her own decisions, and whenever she tried, her mother used guilt to make her submit.

This dynamic carried over into Reya's adult relationships. She dated controlling or overly critical people, much like her mother. When she met Daniel, a charming and confident man, she thought things would be different. But soon, the red flags appeared. Daniel would criticize Reya's decisions, telling her what she should wear or how she should behave. When Reya tried to speak up, Daniel would say, "I'm only looking out for you,"—words that echoed her mother's voice.

At first, Reya didn't recognize the pattern. But after a few months, she started feeling the same way she did with her mother—trapped, powerless, and constantly second-guessing herself. With the support of a close friend, Reya began to see that she had fallen into another controlling relationship.

Breaking free wasn't easy. Reya's conditioning led her to believe that love meant someone taking control of her life. But she slowly began to challenge that belief. She worked with a therapist who helped her understand that true love and care don't involve control—they involve trust, respect, and allowing each other to grow as individuals.

Reya made the tough decision to end her relationship with Daniel. It was a massive step for her, and she felt a sense of relief and freedom for the first time. She wasn't constantly walking on eggshells or worried about disappointing someone.

After the breakup, Reya focused on building healthier relationships, starting with herself. She began listening to her own needs and making decisions that felt right for her, not what others wanted. When she started dating again, she noticed how her new partner treated her. Was there respect?

Could they communicate openly without her feeling manipulated or controlled?

Eventually, Reya found herself in a relationship different from anything she had experienced before. There was no power struggle or need to dominate. Instead, they made decisions together, and Reya felt safe to be herself. For Reya, finding a healthy relationship meant learning to break free from control and reclaiming her right to live on her terms.

Mike: Learning to Trust After a Childhood of Criticism

Mike grew up with a father who was impossible to please. His dad criticized everything Mike did, whether it was his grades, sports performance, or even how he spoke. "You can do better" was a constant refrain. As a result, Mike developed a deep insecurity, constantly feeling like he wasn't good enough.

As an adult, this insecurity followed Mike into his relationships. He felt he had to earn love by being perfect, constantly seeking validation and approval. His romantic relationships were incredibly challenging.

He either dated people who mirrored his father's criticism or people who were emotionally unavailable, reinforcing his belief that he wasn't worthy of love.

Mike's turning point came when his long-term partner broke up, telling him he was too emotionally distant. This feedback hit Mike hard because he thought he had been doing everything right by trying to be the perfect partner. But instead of wallowing in self-pity, Mike decided to get help.

Through therapy, Mike started to understand the impact of his father's criticism on his self-worth. He realized he had been living with a deep fear of rejection, always trying to be "good enough" for others. His therapist helped him see that healthy relationships aren't about perfection or constant approval but trust, vulnerability, and emotional connection.

Mike learned to let down his guard and be more open in his relationships. He started small, sharing his feelings with close friends instead of always putting on a brave face. This openness wasn't effortless, and Mike feared people would judge or think less of him. But to his surprise, the opposite happened. His friends appreciated his honesty, and his relationships deepened.

When Mike eventually started dating again, he approached it differently. He didn't try to be perfect or hide his insecurities. Instead, he allowed himself to be vulnerable and honest. If he felt uncertain or anxious, he communicated it rather than bottling it up. This shift made all the difference. His new partner responded with understanding and reassurance; Mike felt secure in a relationship for the first time.

Mike's journey showed him that healthy relationships aren't about proving your worth but building trust and connection. By learning to trust himself and open up emotionally, Mike formed a relationship that wasn't based on fear or perfection but on mutual respect and love.

The path to healthy relationships wasn't straightforward in the stories of Bina, Reya, and Mike. Each of them had to unlearn toxic patterns from their childhoods, whether it was people-pleasing, accepting control, or seeking perfection. But by setting boundaries, challenging old beliefs, and learning to trust themselves, they found their way to healthier, more fulfilling connections.

Healthy relationships aren't about avoiding conflict or making everyone else happy. They're about balance, mutual respect, and emotional safety. When you've grown up in a toxic family environment, it's hard to believe that these kinds of relationships exist. But with time, self-awareness, and a willingness to change, you can create connections that lift you instead of holding you down.

The Role of Therapy and Self-Help: Healing from Emotional Abuse

When you grow up with narcissistic parents, the damage doesn't end when you leave the house or become an adult. It often follows you into your relationships, your self-esteem, and how you view the world. Therapy, support groups, and self-help are essential tools for healing because they help you untangle the emotional mess caused by years of manipulation, control, and neglect. Let's look at how therapy and self-care transformed the lives of Neha, Arjun, and Zoe.

Neha: Learning to Put Herself First

Neha's mother made her believe that her worth depended on how much she could do for others. Growing up, Neha was the "good daughter" who cared for her mother's needs, managed household responsibilities, and always put her desires last. Her mother's constant guilt-tripping made Neha believe that putting herself first was selfish.

When Neha was in her mid-30s, she felt utterly burned out. She had no energy left for herself because she spent all her time caring for everyone else—her mother, siblings, and even her friends. On top of that, Neha's mother still found ways to criticize her for not doing enough.

This constant cycle of giving and feeling unappreciated was taking a toll on Neha's mental health.

A friend suggested Neha see a therapist. At first, Neha was hesitant. She didn't think she needed help. But after a few sessions, she realized how deeply her childhood affected her. Her therapist helped her understand that her mother's demands and guilt-tripping weren't usual. Neha understood that her value didn't come from what she could do for others but from her intrinsic worth.

One of Neha's most prominent breakthroughs was learning about boundaries. Her therapist taught her that it was okay to say "no" without feeling guilty. It was a foreign concept to Neha, but slowly, she started practicing. She felt anxious and scared the first time she said no to her mother's unreasonable request. But nothing terrible happened. Her mother got upset, but Neha didn't cave in. It was a small victory, but for Neha, it was life-changing.

As she continued therapy, Neha began to focus on self-care. She started setting aside time for things she enjoyed— reading, going for walks, and spending time with friends who genuinely supported her. Self-care became a way for Neha to reconnect with herself, something she hadn't done in years. Neha's story shows how therapy and self-care can help you break the cycle of people-pleasing and guilt that narcissistic parents instil in their children. By setting boundaries and prioritizing her own well-being, Neha learned to take control of her life and reclaim her sense of self.

Arjun: Rebuilding Self-Esteem After Years of Criticism

Arjun grew up with a father who never had a kind word to say. Arjun grew up with a father who never had a kind word to say. Every accomplishment received the response, "You could have done better," and every mistake was exaggerated. By the time Arjun reached adulthood, his father had shattered his self-esteem. He couldn't see his worth and constantly felt like he wasn't good enough.

In his 20s, Arjun struggled with relationships and his career. He found himself in jobs where his bosses were just as critical as his father. Arjun stayed in relationships where his partners belittled him because that was what he was used to. Deep down, Arjun believed he didn't deserve better.

Things changed when Arjun joined a support group for adult children of narcissistic parents. At first, he didn't think it would help. He figured his issues were just his fault. But sitting with others in the room with similar experiences opened his eyes. For the first time, he realized he wasn't alone and that what he went through as a child had a name: emotional abuse.

Hearing others share their stories helped Arjun understand that the criticism he endured growing up didn't reflect his worth. His father's constant belittling wasn't about him; it was about his father's insecurities and need for control.

The support group became a place where Arjun could speak openly about his experiences without fear of judgment. He began to realize that the negative voice in his head—the one telling him he wasn't good enough—wasn't his voice. It was the voice of his father that had taken up space in his mind for years.

With his support group's encouragement, Arjun started rebuilding his self-esteem. He took small steps, like speaking up more at work or standing up for himself in social situations. Each time he challenged that inner voice, he felt a little stronger.

Over time, Arjun's confidence grew. He switched jobs to a company that valued his contributions and treated him with respect. Arjun made it clear how he wanted to be treated in his relationships, and if those expectations weren't met, he chose to leave.

Arjun's healing came from combining therapy and finding a supportive community. People who understood his experiences helped Arjun realize he wasn't broken, and counseling provided him with the tools to rebuild his self-worth.

Zoe: Finding Herself Through Self-Help

Zoe's experience with her narcissistic mother left her feeling lost and confused. Growing up, her mother would use gaslighting tactics, making Zoe question her reality. If Zoe ever pointed out her mother's hurtful behavior, she would hear, "You're overreacting" or "That never happened." As a result, Zoe learned to doubt her own perceptions and feelings.

By the time Zoe was an adult, she struggled with trusting herself. She would second-guess every decision, wondering if she was being "too sensitive" or imagining things. This self-doubt spilled over into her relationships, where she let others dictate her choices because she didn't trust her own judgment.

Zoe had always been an avid reader, so something clicked when she stumbled across a book about narcissistic parents. As she read through the descriptions of gaslighting and emotional manipulation, she recognized her own experiences. For the first time, Zoe had a name for what she went through, and it was a relief.

That book sparked a journey of self-discovery. Zoe started devouring self-help books and articles about healing from narcissistic abuse. While she didn't immediately go to therapy, she found comfort and guidance in the words of experts who had studied this type of trauma.

Through her reading, Zoe learned practical strategies for rebuilding her trust in herself. She started journaling daily, writing down her thoughts and feelings to help her sort through the confusion. Slowly, she began to reconnect with her inner voice.

One of the most helpful exercises for Zoe was practicing self-validation. Each time she made a decision, she would remind herself that her feelings were valid and that she had the right to trust her instincts. At first, it felt unnatural, but over time, it became easier.

Zoe's journey wasn't about a sudden breakthrough but small, consistent changes that helped her rebuild her sense of self. Eventually, she did seek therapy to deepen her healing, but her self-help journey gave her the foundation she needed to start trusting herself again.

Zoe's story shows that self-help can be a powerful tool in healing, especially for those who may not be ready to dive into therapy right away. It gave her the knowledge and tools to understand her experiences and reclaim her trust in herself.

Therapy, support groups, and self-help are all critical pieces in healing from the damage caused by narcissistic parents. Each person's journey looks different—some find healing in one-on-one therapy, others in the shared experiences of support groups, and some through self-help practices. However, all these approaches have in common that they provide a space for understanding, self-reflection, and growth.

Whether you relate to Neha's struggle with boundaries, Arjun's shattered self-esteem, or Zoe's battle with self-doubt, healing is about reclaiming your voice, learning to trust yourself again, and finding the best tools. Healing is possible, and it starts with taking the first step toward understanding and caring for yourself.

Chapter 6: Advancing Towards a Life of Freedom

"Overcoming abuse doesn't just happen; It takes positive steps every day. Let today be the day you start to move forward.

— Assunta Harris

- Self-Love and Acceptance

- Building Emotional Strength and Resilience

- Freedom from the Shadows of Narcissistic Abuse

Self-Acceptance and Self-Care

Breaking Free from External Validation

Being raised by narcissistic parents can lead to constantly seeking approval from others. Whether you sought approval or aimed to dodge disapproval from your parents, you likely realized early on that your value was linked to their opinions of you. This constant need for validation doesn't go away when you grow up. It can seep into every aspect of your life, from relationships to work to how you see yourself. But here's the truth: you don't need anyone else's approval to feel worthy. Learning to accept yourself entirely is a process, but it's the key to breaking free from the patterns narcissistic parents create.

Understanding the Need for External Validation

Let's start with why so many adult children of narcissistic parents feel the need for external validation. Narcissistic parents rarely provide the unconditional love and acceptance that children need to develop a strong sense of self. Instead, they might withhold praise or affection unless you meet their expectations, which could be unrealistic or constantly shifting. As a result, you grow up feeling like you're never quite enough—always chasing after something, whether it's approval, love, or validation.

This pattern can follow you into adulthood. You may find yourself in relationships where you constantly seek reassurance, or you might feel devastated by even the slightest criticism at work. You might spend much time comparing yourself to others, feeling that you must repeatedly prove yourself. But what's happening here is that you're still looking outside of yourself for worth.

The journey to self-love and acceptance means turning that focus inward. It's about recognizing that your value isn't determined by what others think of you or your achievement. It's about knowing that you are enough, just as you are.

Case 1: Bina's Struggle with Perfectionism

Bina grew up with a mother who always found something wrong with what she did. If Bina came home with good grades, her mother would say, "Why didn't you get 100%?" If Bina cleaned the house, her mother would point out the one spot she missed. Nothing was ever enough. As a result, Bina developed perfectionist tendencies. She believed that her mother and others would finally approve of her if she could be perfect.

But perfectionism comes with a price. In her adult life, Bina constantly felt anxious and stressed, trying to be flawless in everything she did. She was terrified of making mistakes because, in her mind, a mistake meant failure, which meant she wasn't good enough.

It wasn't until Bina started therapy that she began to see the pattern. Her therapist pointed out how Bina was chasing an impossible standard and asked her a question that stuck with her: "What would happen if you weren't perfect?"

At first, Bina resisted the idea. She thought that if she let go of her need to be perfect, everything would fall apart. However, through therapy, Bina slowly started experimenting with being kinder to herself. She allowed herself to make small mistakes and didn't rush to fix them. Bina eventually grasped that her self-worth didn't depend on achieving perfection. She was worthy simply because she existed.

Bina's story shows how deeply ingrained the need for external validation can be, but it also indicates that breaking free from it is possible. By learning to accept herself—flaws and all—Bina found a sense of peace she had never experienced before.

Case 2: Reya's Journey to Self-Acceptance

Reya grew up feeling invisible. Her father was the type of narcissist who didn't criticize her openly, but he also ignored her. She often felt like she had to compete for his love and approval, but no matter what she did, it never seemed to make a difference. Reya carried this feeling of invisibility into adulthood. She would often downplay her accomplishments or stay quiet in social settings, thinking that no one really cared about her opinion.

In relationships, Reya struggled with a fear of abandonment. She would stay in situations that weren't good for her to avoid being alone. Deep down, she believed she wouldn't be good enough if someone left her. Despite not feeling worthy herself, she constantly tried to prove her worth.

Reya's turning point came when she joined a support group for people healing from narcissistic abuse. For the first time, she met others who had been through similar experiences, and hearing their stories helped her realize she wasn't alone. In the group, Reya learned about self-compassion—treating herself with the kindness she would offer a friend. Initially, this was a foreign concept because she was so used to being hard on herself.

As Reya began to practice self-compassion, she noticed a shift in how she felt about herself. She started acknowledging her own achievements, no matter how small, and stopped relying on others to validate her. She realized that her worth wasn't dependent on how others treated her or whether they stayed in her life. It was something that came from within.

Self-acceptance didn't happen overnight for Reya. It took time, patience, and a lot of inner work. But the more she focused on nurturing herself, the more confident and secure she felt. Today, Reya no longer feels the need to prove herself to others. She knows she is enough, just as she is.

Case 3: Mike's Realization That He Deserves Better

Mike's mother was the type of narcissist who played the victim. She always made Mike feel guilty for wanting anything for himself. If he spent time with his friends, she would say, "I guess I'm not important to you anymore." She would accuse him of being selfish and uncaring if he set boundaries.

When Mike was in his 40s, he had developed a pattern of putting others' needs before his own. He often found himself in one-sided relationships, where he gave and gave but rarely got anything in return. Mike believed that if he kept everyone else happy, he would eventually get the love and appreciation he sought.

It wasn't until Mike had a significant burnout that he realized something had to change. He was constantly exhausted, emotionally drained, and resentful. A close friend suggested he see a therapist, and that's when Mike began to unpack the ways his upbringing had shaped his behavior.

In therapy, Mike learned about boundaries—something he had never thought about before. He realized it was okay to say no and that taking care of himself wasn't selfish. Slowly, Mike began to set boundaries with the people in his life, including his mother.

At first, it wasn't easy. Mike's mother reacted with guilt trips and emotional manipulation, but this time, he didn't fall for it. He had learned to recognize these tactics for what they were, and instead of feeling guilty, he focused on his own well-being. Through therapy, Mike learned to prioritize his needs and, most importantly, to validate himself. Mike's journey shows that even after years of putting others first, it's never too late to start prioritizing yourself. By recognizing his worth and setting boundaries, Mike learned that he didn't need anyone else's approval to feel deserving of love and respect.

Learning to Love and Accept Yourself

Whether it's Bina's struggle with perfectionism, Reya's fear of abandonment, or Mike's battle with guilt, the common thread is the need for external validation. Narcissistic parents often teach their children that they are only worthy if they meet certain expectations or serve a specific purpose. But real healing comes when you learn to turn that validation inward.

Loving and accepting yourself means acknowledging that you are enough just as you are. You don't need to be perfect, and you don't need to prove yourself to anyone. It's about giving yourself the compassion, kindness, and understanding you may not have received from your parents.

This journey isn't easy, and it doesn't happen overnight. But as you learn to value yourself, you'll find the need for external validation fades. You'll realize that your worth isn't something others give you—it's something that's always been inside you.

Building Resilience and Emotional Strength: Protecting Yourself from Future Toxic

When you grow up with narcissistic parents, your emotional resilience takes a hit. Walking on eggshells to avoid their disapproval can result in self-doubt. The emotional impact of being raised in this environment doesn't just go away when you become an adult—it follows you. As a result, you might find yourself in toxic relationships, drawn to people who reflect the unhealthy dynamics you grew up with. But the good news is you can build resilience and emotional strength so you don't fall into these traps again.

Let's talk about some practical tools to help you maintain emotional balance and avoid future toxic relationships. It starts with understanding your patterns, setting boundaries, and, most importantly, strengthening your self-worth.

Understanding Your Patterns

Building resilience begins with acknowledging the patterns that have emerged from your upbringing. Children of narcissistic parents often end up in relationships with people who mirror their parents' behavior, which is not a coincidence. How you were raised has influenced your understanding of what is normal or acceptable.

For example, if your parent was overly critical, you might be drawn to a partner who also criticizes you because it feels familiar. You might not notice how damaging it is because it's what you've always known. Or, if your parent was emotionally unavailable, you might find yourself attracted to people who are distant or cold, thinking you can win them over if you try hard enough.

The key here is awareness. You need to take a step back and look at your past relationships. Do you notice any patterns? Are you repeatedly drawn to people who are controlling, manipulative, or emotionally unavailable? You can begin to change these patterns once you start to see them. It's about breaking the cycle and choosing healthier relationships.

Establishing Limits

Well-defined peripheries help you from toxic people. Narcissistic parents often ignore or violate boundaries, leaving their children confused about what's acceptable and what isn't. Perhaps you were raised with the idea that saying "no" is selfish or that your needs are less important than those of others. As a result, you might struggle to set boundaries in your adult relationships.

But boundaries are essential for emotional health. They tell others how you expect to be treated, and, more importantly, they protect your emotional space. Without clear boundaries, toxic people will take advantage of your kindness or manipulate you into doing things that aren't in your best interest.

Setting boundaries doesn't mean you have to be harsh or aggressive. It's about being transparent and firm about what you tolerate and won't tolerate. For example, if someone always puts you down, you can assertively state, "I won't tolerate being spoken to in that manner." If it continues, I'll have to distance myself from this relationship." It's not about changing the other person's behavior—it's about protecting yourself and deciding what's acceptable.

The more you practice setting boundaries, the more natural it will feel. You'll start noticing how empowering it is to take control of your emotional space and prevent toxic people from crossing the line.

Strengthening Your Sense of Self-Worth

One of the most damaging things about growing up with narcissistic parents is the erosion of self-worth. You may have experienced feeling inadequate despite your best efforts.

It leaves you vulnerable to seeking validation from others, especially in relationships. When you don't feel good about yourself, you're more likely to tolerate toxic behavior because you believe you don't deserve better.

Building resilience means strengthening your sense of self-worth. You need to know, deep down, that you are worthy of love, respect, and healthy relationships. It's not an instant process, but there are things you can do to boost your self-confidence.

Positive Self-Talk: Pay attention to the way you talk to yourself. If you constantly criticize yourself or doubt your abilities, you reinforce the negative messages you received growing up. Start replacing those thoughts with positive affirmations. Instead of saying, "I'm not good enough," try saying, "I am enough just as I am." It might initially feel awkward, but these positive statements will become more natural.

Celebrate Small Wins

 Building self-worth is about acknowledging your progress, even the tiny things. Did you set a boundary with someone? That's a win. Did you speak up for yourself at work? Another win. These victories might seem small, but they add up. By celebrating them, you're reinforcing the idea that you are capable and worthy.

Surround Yourself with Supportive People

Your environment plays a significant role in how you feel about yourself. It will be harder to build your self-worth if you're constantly around people who tear you down. Seek out relationships with people who support you, encourage you, and appreciate you for who you are. The more you surround yourself with positivity, the stronger your sense of self will become.

Managing Emotional Triggers

Children of narcissistic parents often carry emotional triggers from their past. These situations or behaviors bring up old feelings of hurt, rejection, or inadequacy. For example, if someone criticizes you, it might remind you of how your parent used to blame you, and you'll react more intensely than the situation warrants.

Learning to manage these triggers is a crucial part of building emotional strength. Identifying when you're triggered is the initial step. Pay attention to your body and emotions. Do you suddenly feel anxious or angry when someone says something critical? That's a clue that something's bringing up a past hurt.

If you feel triggered, remember to pause for a moment. Breathe deeply and remind yourself that this situation is different from your past. You are no longer a child at the mercy of a narcissistic parent. You have the power to choose how to respond. Practice mindfulness, stay grounded to manage your emotional reactions, and prevent old wounds from controlling your behavior.

Cultivating Emotional Resilience

Building resilience means bouncing back from emotional setbacks without letting them destroy your sense of self. It's about handling life's challenges without falling apart or turning to unhealthy coping mechanisms.

One of the best ways to build emotional resilience is through self-care. It isn't just about pampering yourself with bubble baths or spa days (though those can be nice, too). It's about ensuring you care for your mental, emotional, and physical health.

Physical self-care could mean getting enough sleep, eating nutritious foods, and exercising regularly.

Mental self-care might involve journaling, practicing mindfulness, and pursuing the hobbies that bring you joy.

Emotional self-care could mean seeking support from your dear ones, such as a therapist, or joining a support group where you can share your experiences and gain insights from others.

Another key to emotional resilience is learning how to manage stress. Life will always have stressful moments, but how you respond to stress can make all the difference. Techniques like deep breathing, meditation, and yoga can help you stay calm in facing challenges.

Building resilience and emotional strength is a process that requires time and effort, but it's worth it. By understanding your patterns, setting boundaries, strengthening your sense of self-worth, and practicing self-care, you can protect yourself from toxic relationships in the future. You no longer have to live under the shadow of your past. You have the power to break free, rebuild your life, and cultivate healthy, fulfilling relationships.

It's important to remember that building resilience doesn't mean you'll never feel pain or hurt again. But it does mean you'll have the tools to handle those emotions and bounce back stronger. Over time, you'll find that the toxic relationships that once seemed so familiar no longer have a place in your life. Instead, you'll create space for people who genuinely value and respect you—and that's where true emotional strength comes from.

Living Free from the Shadows of Narcissistic Abuse

When you've grown up with a narcissistic parent, the effects linger long after childhood. Many people don't even realize how much of their adult life is shaped by those early experiences. It's like living in a shadow you didn't choose, a constant reminder of pain, self-doubt, and emotional manipulation. But there's a way out, and it starts with recognizing the damage and then deciding to break free.

This chapter will examine how you can envision and build a fulfilling life where your past does not define you. Through the stories of Bina, Reya, and Mike, we'll see how people just like you have learned to live free from the shadows of narcissistic abuse.

Case 1: Bina's Story—Letting Go of Guilt

Bina was in her late thirties when she finally acknowledged the emotional toll her mother had taken on her life. Growing up, her mother controlled every aspect of her day—what she wore, what she studied, even who her friends were. Whenever Bina tried to show her independence, she faced guilt-inducing remarks such as, "After everything I've done for you, is this how you thank me?"

Bina's relationships reflected this struggle. She dated emotionally unavailable people, yet she always tried to win their approval, just as she had with her mother. She worked in a career her mother had chosen for her despite not feeling passionate about it. Whenever Bina thought about changing jobs or moving away to start fresh, her mother's voice echoed in her mind, making her feel like she'd be abandoning the family.

The breakthrough for Bina came when she started therapy. Her therapist helped her see that the guilt she carried wasn't hers—it was something her mother had implanted in her to keep control. Understanding this was a huge relief. Slowly, Bina learned to relinquish the guilt and began practicing saying "no" to her mother's demands. It wasn't easy. Every time Bina stood up for herself, the guilt would creep back in, but she learned to recognize it as a tool of manipulation, not a reflection of her true feelings.

Today, Bina is living a much more accessible life. She's in a relationship with someone who respects her boundaries and is exploring new career options that align with her passions. Bina's journey teaches us that letting go of guilt is one of the first steps to living free from the shadow of narcissistic abuse.

Case 2: Reya's Story—Rebuilding Self-Esteem

Her father's constant criticism marked Reya's childhood. No matter what she did, it was never good enough. He'd find a flaw if she brought home a school project she was proud of. He'd remind her of what she hadn't done yet if she achieved something. As a consequence, Reya developed the belief that she couldn't accomplish a lot. Her father's voice became her inner critic, always pointing out her failures and diminishing her successes.

As an adult, Reya struggled with low self-esteem. She second-guessed herself in every situation—at work, in friendships, and even in mundane tasks like choosing what to wear. She sought validation from others because she couldn't find it within herself, leading to being in relationships where she was undervalued and overlooked.

It wasn't until Reya started journaling about her feelings that she realized how deeply her father's voice had become her own. Despite her achievements, she dismissed them in her writing due to internalized inadequacy. It made her realize that the self-doubt didn't originate from within her; it reflected her father's constant criticism.

Reya decided to take small steps toward rebuilding her self-esteem. Every day, she made a point to acknowledge something she had done well, no matter how small. She also surrounded herself with supportive people who celebrated her accomplishments instead of tearing her down. Over time, Reya's inner critic became quieter, and she found herself feeling more confident and capable.

Reya's story shows us that rebuilding self-esteem after narcissistic abuse isn't about making massive changes overnight. It's about recognizing and gradually replacing your internalized negative beliefs with positive, affirming ones. Reya has gained confidence in her identity and no longer allows her self-worth to be defined by her father's opinions.

In Case 3, Mike's experience focuses on implementing boundaries for the first time.

Mike's father was charismatic, but beneath the charm was a controlling, manipulative person who expected complete obedience from his children. Mike learned early on that his father's approval came with a price—he had to give up his own needs and desires to keep the peace. His father insisted on loyalty, making Mike's effort to assert independence perceived as betrayal. As a result, Mike grew up without ever learning to set boundaries.

In his adult life, Mike struggled with people-pleasing. At work, he took on extra projects he didn't have time for because he didn't know how to say no. In friendships, Mike let others dictate the terms, often going along with things that made him uncomfortable.

He avoided conflict at all costs in relationships, even when it meant ignoring his needs.

Things changed when Mike attended a support group for adult children of narcissistic parents. Hearing others talk about their experiences helped him see he wasn't alone, giving him the courage to set boundaries. Initially, Mike took a small step by turning down an invitation to an event he had no interest in attending, a situation which he would have normally felt obliged to accept. It felt uncomfortable initially, but the more Mike practiced setting boundaries, the more empowered he felt.

Mike's biggest challenge came when he decided to confront his father. He didn't expect his father to change, but Mike knew he needed to draw a line to protect his own mental health. He calmly explained that he wouldn't tolerate the manipulation anymore. Predictably, his father tried to guilt him into compliance, but Mike stood firm. For the first time, Mike felt he had control over his relationship with his father.

Setting boundaries doesn't always lead to dramatic confrontations. For Mike, it started with small, everyday decisions where he prioritized his needs over others' demands. Over time, these small steps added up, and Mike was able to reclaim his sense of autonomy.

Progressing Ahead—Actions You Can Implement

The stories of Bina, Reya, and Mike show us that living free from the shadows of narcissistic abuse is a process. It doesn't happen overnight, and it's not about waiting for a magical healing moment. It's about small, consistent steps that help you reclaim your life, bit by bit.

Here are some practical steps you can take:

Recognize the Patterns

Like Bina, you need to understand how your narcissistic parent's behavior still affects you. Whether it's guilt, self-doubt, or people-pleasing, awareness is the first step toward change.

Set Boundaries

Mike's journey shows boundaries are essential for protecting your emotional health. Start small if needed, but don't be afraid to stand up for yourself.

Rebuild Self-Esteem

Like Reya, you may need to work on seeing your worth, and it can be as simple as acknowledging your accomplishments and surrounding yourself with supportive people.

Seek Support: Whether through therapy, support groups, or trusted friends, don't be afraid to lean on others as you work through your healing process. You don't have to do it alone.

Patience is a must

Healing from narcissistic abuse takes time. There will be setbacks, but every small step forward is progress.

Living free from the shadows of narcissistic abuse means taking control of your life and not letting the past define you. It's about building a life that feels authentic and fulfilling, where you set the terms of your relationships and treat yourself with the respect you deserve.

Do you wonder if Bina, Reya, and Mike have the ability? It's never too late to break free and create a life that reflects your true self, not the version of you that your narcissistic parent wanted to control. You can live without their shadows, taking it one step at a time.

Important Points from Each Chapter

Chapter 1: Understanding Narcissistic Parental Abuse

- Narcissistic parents often control, manipulate, and prioritize their own needs over their children's.
- Children of narcissistic parents may feel unloved or only valued for what they can provide.
- The family dynamic often includes roles like "scapegoat" or "golden child," leading to sibling rivalry.
- Sons and daughters may experience the abuse differently but suffer similar emotional harm.
- Recognizing the signs of narcissistic maternal abuse is the first step toward healing.

Chapter 2: The Deep Wounds of Childhood

- Constant criticism and manipulation damage a child's self-esteem and identity.
- Narcissistic parents make their children feel responsible for their emotions, creating guilt and shame.

- Children of narcissists often grow up feeling afraid, anxious, or unable to trust others.
- To cope, many children learn to hide their emotions or become people-pleasers.
- Addressing these deep emotional wounds in adulthood is necessary as they don't heal independently.

Chapter 3: Carrying the Scars into Adulthood

- Adult survivors often struggle with low self-worth and may attract toxic relationships.
- The emotional scars from childhood can lead to anxiety, depression, or difficulty forming healthy connections.
- Many survivors unconsciously seek narcissistic partners, repeating the cycle of abuse.
- Emotional triggers from childhood can resurface in adult life, causing distress.
- Understanding how these scars affect adult life is essential for breaking free from past trauma.

Chapter 4: Breaking the Cycle

- Healing starts with recognizing and admitting the impact of narcissistic abuse.
- Setting clear boundaries with a narcissistic mother is crucial in protecting your emotional well-being.
- Healing the "inner child" helps in addressing deep-rooted pain from childhood.
- Breaking the cycle requires unlearning toxic patterns and developing healthier habits.
- Moving forward with self-care, therapy, and a support system is possible.

Chapter 5: Rebuilding Your Life After Trauma

- Reclaiming your self-worth is the first step in rebuilding your life after narcissistic abuse.
- The key to healthy relationships is mutual respect, not control or manipulation.
- Therapy, support groups, and self-care are essential tools for recovery.
- Learning to trust yourself and others again takes time, but it's achievable with patience.
- Healing isn't just about survival but thriving and finding joy.

Chapter 6: Moving Forward—A Life of Freedom

- Self-love and acceptance are crucial for moving forward and letting go of the past.
- Building emotional resilience helps you cope with future challenges and avoid toxic relationships.
- You can create a fulfilling life by focusing on your own needs and happiness, not others' expectations.
- It is possible to live free from the shadows of narcissistic abuse with conscious effort and support.
- Freedom from past trauma allows you to live authentically and confidently in your own skin.

Disclaimer

The purpose of the information in "Narcissistic Parental Abuse Recovery" is informational and educational only. This book does not substitute professional medical, psychological, or legal advice. We encourage readers experiencing emotional or psychological distress related to narcissistic parental abuse to seek the support of licensed therapists, counselors, or other qualified professionals.

This book's experiences, examples, and case studies are based on common patterns and may not reflect every individual's situation. While I have strived for accuracy and relevance in the information provided, readers should still consider their individual situations when using the guidance given.

The author and publisher absolve themselves of any responsibility for risks, losses, or damages arising from using the information in this book. Healing from narcissistic parental abuse is a deeply personal journey, and progress varies from person to person.

Reference

1. https://www.pinkgirlteaches.com/post/facing-the-pain-deception-rejection-and-intrusive-thoughts-after-narcissistic-abuse
2. https://www.stylecraze.com/articles/selfish-parents-quotes/
3. https://www.bulbapp.io/p/6f6f32e3-7d0e-4903-9ee1-eaa5a39af76d/toxic-tango-dealing-with-a-partners-bad-attitude
4. https://www.restonyc.com/will-i-ever-recover-from-narcissistic-abuse/
5. https://weirdlysuccessful.org/adaptations/
6. https://www.uptickerapp.com/post/balancing-act-how-to-find-harmony-between-work-and-personal-life
7. https://christandpopculture.com/brilliant-lost-children-the-familiar-roots-of-elena-ferrantes-neapolitan-novels/
8. https://www.webmd.com/mental-health/narcissism-symptoms-signs the pathological narcissist's lack of empathy.
9. https://alineacenter.com/nashville-narcissism/
10. https://humanbehaviorlab.com/3-signs-you-are-in-the-presence-of-a-narcissist/
11. https://maxmymoney.org/narcissistic-parents-are-the-worst-15-behaviors-they-passed-down-to-you/
12. https://mindpsychiatrist.com/how-to-tell-if-you-re-with-a-narcissist/
13. "Journal of Alternative Medicine Research, vol. 15, no. 2, 2023, pp. 197-208.

A Note of Gratitude

Dear Reader,

Thank you for choosing Narcissistic Parental Abuse Recovery and for taking this step toward healing. Your decision to read this book shows courage, and I'm genuinely grateful to be part of your journey. It will help you and your dear ones get guidance. This book supports you, and I encourage you to use it as much as you need. Revisit sections, take notes, and reflect on what resonates with you. Healing is a process, and I hope that this book becomes a helpful companion along the way.

I'd also like to invite you to explore other books in my other series, where I discuss related topics and offer guidance for personal growth and recovery from emotional abuse. Each book published in the other two series, "Natural Health and Alternative Healing" and "Cognitive Mastery," will help you achieve the same goal: success and empowerment.

Please visit my website: https://aruhoskeri.in and
My Amazon Author Central Page:
https://www.amazon.com/author/dr_arundhati-hoskeri
Thank you for your time and trust. Wishing you strength, peace, and a fulfilling journey forward.

Warm regards,
Dr Arundhati Hoskeri

Contact Email: authorarug@gmail.com

About the Author

Dr Arundhati G Hoskeri

MSc (Zoology), MEd, Ph.D., MSc (Clinical Psychology), MA (English), ACTL Diploma in Public Speaking
NDHS (Doctor of Natural Health Sciences)
Certified Cyber Crime Intervention Officer (CCIO)
Educational Consultant for Cambridge International School

Former Director and Principal of Cambridge International School and I B World School

A lifelong learner, Author, Poet, Passionate Educator, Counselor, Natural Health Science Expert, Motivational Speaker, and Freelance Journalist.

Dr Arundhati Hoskeri is a remarkable individual whose passion for learning and educational commitments has defined her illustrious journey. With an unquenchable thirst for knowledge, she has obtained master's degrees in three distinct subjects, a testament to her dedication to intellectual growth. Her academic journey culminated in attaining a Ph.D. in education, reflecting her deep-seated desire to contribute meaningfully to the field.

Throughout her impressive career spanning 37 years, Dr. Arundhati has been a trailblazer in education. Her leadership acumen shines through her role as the head of a prestigious IB (International Baccalaureate) World School and Cambridge International School for over two decades. This extensive experience underscores her exceptional ability to shape and nurture future generations.

Beyond her role as an educator, Dr Arundhati's versatile talents extend into various domains. She is a gifted educator and a practitioner of natural health sciences, earning the title of a Natural Health Science (NDHS) doctor. Her communication prowess is evident in her ACTL Diploma in Public Speaking from Trinity College of London, which has undoubtedly played a pivotal role in her success as a **speaker, educator, and writer.**

Dr Arundhati's impact reaches far beyond the classroom. Her accomplishments as a poet have garnered recognition on national and international platforms, including in countries like India, Sri Lanka, and Malaysia. Her thought-provoking contributions to journalism have graced the pages of esteemed national and international magazines and newspapers, establishing her as a credible voice on various subjects.

As an avid reader and extensive researcher, Dr Arundhati's intellectual curiosity has resulted in the publication of many research articles in esteemed educational journals and conferences—her ability to combine academia with practical insights positions her as **a thought leader** in her field. Her compassion and **dedication to holistic well-being** are evident in her motivational speaker and healer role, where she uses her expertise to promote natural healing, **alternative medicine, emotional healing, and positive transformation**.

Accolades and recognition are a testament to her unwavering commitment and exemplary contributions that mark Dr Arundhati's versatile journey. Her presence as a moderator, keynote speaker, and presenter in national and international seminars has solidified her status as a respected voice in various forums. Dr Arundhati lends her expertise as a consultant to upcoming and established

Cambridge International School, further impacting the education sector with her wealth of knowledge.

Notably, her journey as an author takes center stage, focusing on mental well-being, physical health, and the intricate nuances of human behavior. Her writing endeavors are a testament to her dedication to empowering individuals with practical insights and actionable advice.

Dr Arundhati Govind Hoskeri's legacy has a profound impact and unwavering dedication. Her multifaceted contributions to education, physical and mental health, writing, and motivational speaking continue to inspire and uplift individuals across the globe, glowing through her accomplishments and sincerity.

She always acknowledges the support of her loving family, especially her husband, Dr Govind N Hoskeri, who has been a driving force behind her success and achievements.

Made in the USA
Middletown, DE
02 December 2024